EXPLORING THE PHILIPPINES

EXPLORING THE PHILIPPINES

NIGEL HICKS

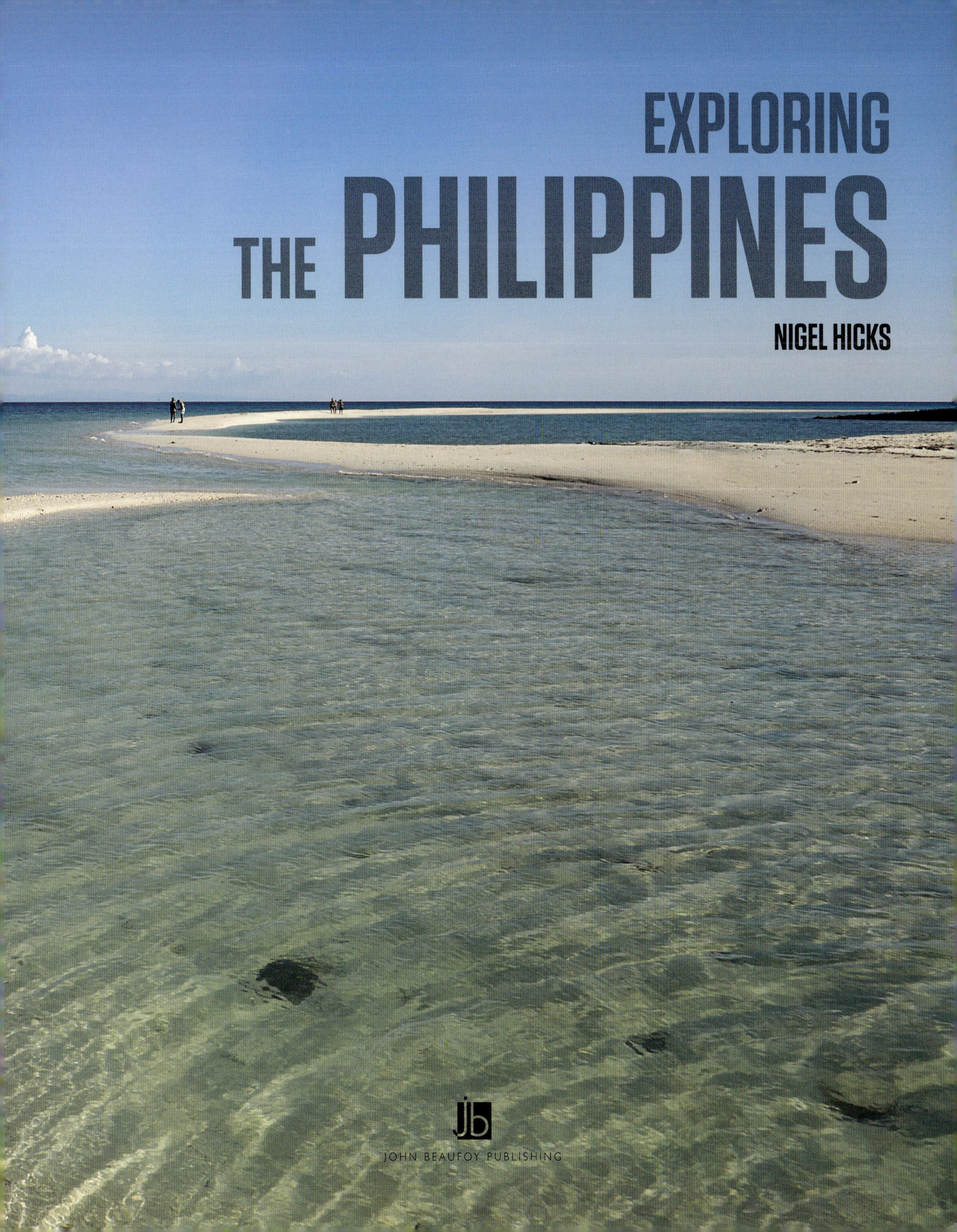

JOHN BEAUFOY PUBLISHING

ACKNOWLEDGEMENTS

Nigel Hicks would like to extend a huge thank you to the following organisations, without whose help this project would have been much harder to accomplish.

The Tourism Promotions Board Philippines (TPB)
The Philippines Department of Tourism, London office
Philippine Airlines, London office
The Golden Phoenix Hotel, Manila
The Diamond Hotel, Manila
The Little Surfmaid Resort, San Juan, La Union.
Club Paradise, Dimakya Island, Busuanga
Costabella Tropical Beach Hotel, Mactan Island, Cebu
The Office of the Mayor of Zamboanga City
Baron Travel

This edition published in the United Kingdom in 2024 by John Beaufoy Publishing,
11 Blenheim Court, 316 Woodstock Road, Oxford OX2 7NS, England
www.johnbeaufoy.com

Previously published as *Journey Through the Philippines*

ISBN 978-1-913679-61-3

Designed by Glyn Bridgewater
Cover design by Ginny Zeal
Cartography by William Smuts
Project management by Rosemary Wilkinson

Printed and bound in Malaysia by Times Offset (M) Sdn. Bhd.

Opposite: Arguably the most popular visitor attraction in the Calamian Islands, the northernmost part of Palawan, is the stunning Kayangan Lake, on Coron Island. Here, boats tie up in the equally beautiful nearby cove, bringing a steady stream of visitors from Coron Town on nearby Busuanga Island.

Title page: The sand bar on Sugar Beach, at Santa Fe, on the south-east coast of Bantayan Island, off the northern tip of Cebu, in the Visayas.

Contents page: A lovely dusk over Coron Bay and the rocky outline of Coron Island, seen from Mt Tapyas, a steep hill that towers above Coron Town on Busuanga Island, in the Calamian group of islands in northern Palawan.

CONTENTS

INTRODUCTION

Travelling through the Philippines is always a memorable experience, particularly when moving around by boat or bus. The boats, buses, towns and harbours are always colourful and lively, ensuring that every journey is packed with energy, action and adventure: there really is hardly a dull moment.

Some of the sleek, modern, long-distance buses and high-speed ferries may lack some character – though at least they are usually comfortable – but it is when you come to be on one of the slower country buses, jeepneys or the *banca* ferries that you really start to experience the Philippines. The buses and jeepneys have all of rural life coming and going on and off them, usually carried out against a backdrop of loud rock music pumping out from the vehicle's sound system. On the *bancas* all sound is drowned out by the roar of the engines, the experience instead becoming largely visual, the brightly painted boat against the blue sky and azure sea, topped off by the occasional sprinkling of salt spray – actually, sometimes a dousing – as the outriggers thump into oncoming waves.

You can travel round pretty much the whole of the Philippines in this way, though the airline network comes in very handy for saving time and energy, particularly when it comes to crossing some of the bigger stretches of water that divide up this sprawling island nation. So in putting together a journey through the Philippines, unless you have oodles of time and patience, a judicious combination of land, sea and air transport will get you around a good selection of the Philippines' most beautiful and most interesting places in a manageable amount of time, while still ensuring that the journey itself is an experience to be savoured and remembered for all the right reasons.

PLANNING A TRIP

But in a vast archipelago of over 7,000 islands, with environments that range from stunning submarine coral reefs to rugged and overly-active volcanoes, with beaches, lakes, rivers and forests in between, plus urban settings that range from highly modern to historic Spanish relics, where on earth do you start?

Clearly, it is just not possible to go everywhere and to do it all. You need to be selective, picking out those places likely to be of most interest to you, while at the same time giving a good cross-section of the sights and experiences that the Philippines has to offer. You could concentrate on going to just the most famous places, but then why would you simply follow the crowd? Instead, be a little inventive and adventurous, and aim to include a selection of places that are at least a little off the beaten track, places that once you have reached them give you a sense of achievement.

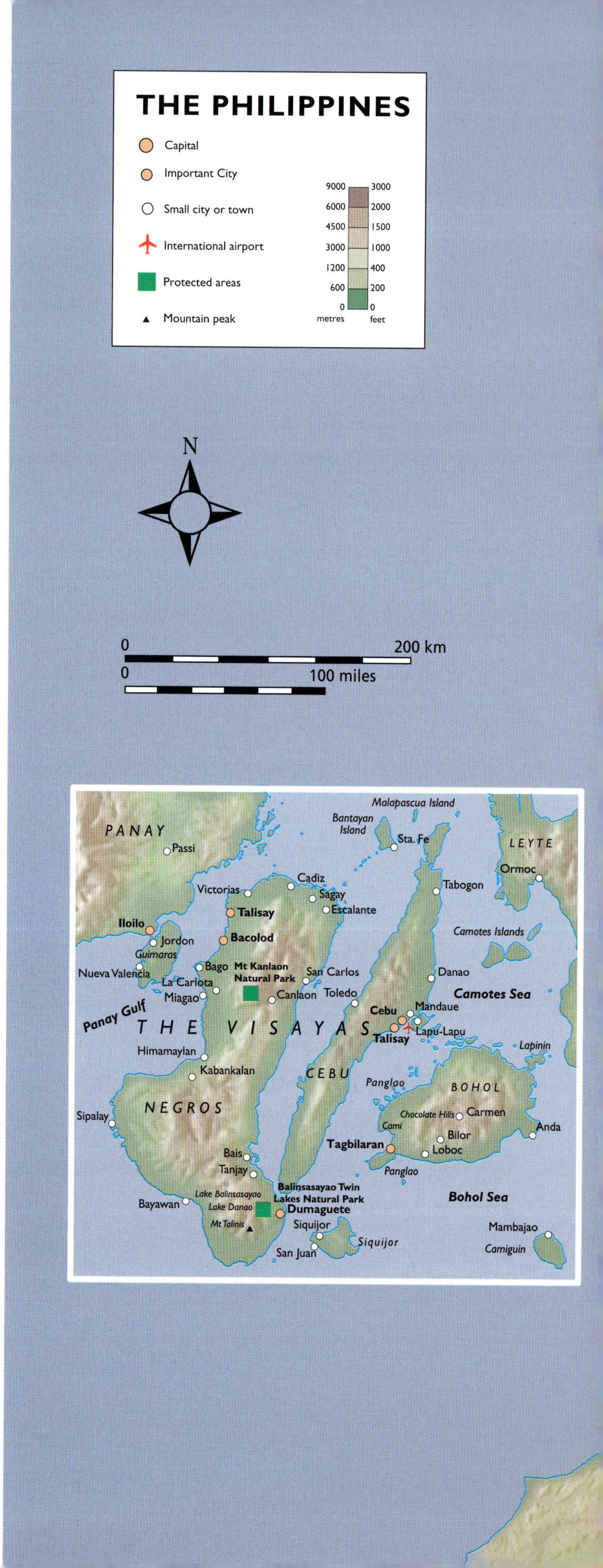

Luzon Strait
Itbayat
Batanes Islands
Batan
PACIFIC
OCEAN
Babuyan
Calayan
Babuyan Islands
Dalupiri
Fuga
Camiguin
Mayraira Point
Pagudpud
Aparri
Cape Engaño
Laoag
Paoay
Bangued
Vigan
CORDILLERA CENTRAL
Cagayan
SIERRA MADRE MTS
Tuguegarao
Northern Sierra Madre Natural Park
Bontoc
Ilagan
Banaue
Cauayan
San Juan
Mt Pulag
San Fernando
Mt Pulag National Park
Solano
Hundred Islands National Park
Baguio
Lingayen Bay
LUZON
Alaminos
Dagupan
Lingayen
Urdaneta
ZAMBALES MTS
San Carlos
Bongabon
Baler Bay
Baler
San Jose
Tarlac
Cabanatuan
Iba
Gapan
Angeles
Mt Pinatubo
San Fernando
Olongapo
Malolos
Polillo Islands
Subic Bay
Manila Bay
Quezon City
Manila
Balanga
Laguna de Bay
PHILIPPINE SEA
Daet
Tagaytay
Taal Lake
San Pablo
Lubang Islands
Balayan Bay
Batangas
Tayabas Bay
Lopez
Ragay Gulf
Naga
Catanduanes
Virac
Mt Mayon
Tabaco
Lagonoy Gulf
Puerto Galera
Legazpi
Rapu Rapu Island
Mt Malasimbo
Boac
Calapan
Marinduque
Donsol
Burias
MINDORO
Sorsogon
Apo Reef Marine Natural Park
Sibuyan
Mt Bulusan
Bulusan Volcano National Park
Laoang
Calamian Group
Mindoro Strait
Romblon
Calauit National Park
Busuanga Group
Tablas Strait
Sibuyan
Masbate
Sea
Tablas
Samar Sea
Calbayog
Culion
Coron
Masbate
SAMAR
Culion Island
Boracay
Visayan Sea
Linapacan Strait
Biliran
Sohoton National Park
Kalibo
Roxas
Bantayan Island
PANAY
El Nido
Passi
Ormoc
Tacloban
Cadiz
Taytay
Cuyo Islands
San Jose de Buenavista
Talisay
LEYTE
Leyte Gulf
Iloilo
Bacolod
San Carlos
Danao
Baybay
Dumaran
Miagao
Jordon
CEBU
Camotes Sea
Guimaras
Mt Kanlaon Natural Park
Cebu
Dinagat
Palawan Passage
Sabang
Puerto Princesa Subterranean River National Park
Talisay
Lapu-Lapu
Maasin
Panay Gulf
THE VISAYAS
Del Carmen
Siargao
Puerto Princesa
General Luna
BOHOL
Sipalay
NEGROS
Anda
Surigao
Dapa
Apurahuan
Tagbilaran
Tanjay
Panglao
Bohol Sea
PALAWAN
Bayawan
Dumaguete
Mambajao
Camiguin
Mt Hibok-Hibok
Tubbataha Reef National Marine Park
Siquijor
Butuan
Gingoog
Lianga
SULU
Dapitan
Bayugan
Dipolog
El Salvador
Cagayan de Oro
SEA
Iligan
Ozamiz
Mt Kitanglad Range Natural Park
Marawi
Balabac
Pagadian
Lake Lanao
Baganga
Balabac Strait
MINDANAO
Tagum
Illana Bay
Malagos
Cotabato
Mati
Davao
Mt Apo
Mapin
Moro Gulf
Mt Apo Natural Park
Zamboanga
Datu Piang
Digos
Davao Gulf
Isabela
Lais
Pangutaran Group
Samales Group
General Santos
Jolo
SULU ARCHIPELAGO
Batulaki
Tapul Group
CELEBES SEA
Balut
Sarangani
Tawitawi Group
MALAYSIA

Right: The steep rice terraces of Batad, a World Heritage Site near Banaue, in the Cordillera Central mountains of northern Luzon.

Opposite: A dusk view along Roxas Boulevard, which runs along the shore of Manila Bay in the Ermite and Malate districts of central Manila, the nation's capital.

Below: Lively and colourful festivals are a major feature of Philippine life, and it is hard to travel around the country without running into a few. This image shows a participant in one of the Philippines' biggest events: Dinagyang, held every January in the Visayan city of Iloilo.

You may be someone who likes nothing better than stomping around on the Philippines' mountains, so include some of that, but not too much. Those rainforests can get pretty damp and claustrophobic, not to mention just plain exhausting. So head for the beaches and chill out, perhaps combined with a touch of snorkelling or diving on those wonderful reefs, as well as some surfing on those great waves. But again don't do too much of the beach thing either: simply hopping from one strip of dazzlingly beautiful white coral sand to another can make you lazy, and you would not want that. Then of course there is the urban scene, a touch of culture in the museums and historic sites to bring you back into line with the Philippines' past and present after all that beach and mountain fun, followed by a dose of hedonism in the bars, cafés and restaurants to soften the impact of the culture.

Once you have successfully put together a plan that covers a touch of the best of everything, suddenly you have a journey through the Philippines. That is exactly what this book does for you: it presents a journey through 30 locations across the country, running roughly from north to south, taking in many of the best sites encompassing the enormous diversity found throughout the Philippines. Some of the country's most famous locations are included, places that are firmly on the beaten track. These include not only Manila and Cebu City of course, but also the island resort of Boracay, the famous rice terraces of Banaue and the mountain capital that is Baguio. Other locations are only lightly visited, places such as the beaches of Pagudpud, Baler and Siquijor, the mountain retreat of Sagada, and the volcanoes of southern Bicol. What they all have in common is that they represent some of the best that the Philippines has to offer, places that are all really worth visiting in any journey through the Philippines. Read on and enjoy the journey.

LUZON

THE MAIN HUB OF THE PHILIPPINES

Our journey starts in Luzon, the Philippine heartland, and specifically on its northernmost shores around the resorts of Pagudpud and the city of Laoag. From here the mostly southward journey takes in a huge variety of sites that really sums up the diversity of the whole of the Philippines. These range from historic towns (Vigan and Taal) through beach, island and surfing centres (San Juan, Hundred Islands and Baler), mountain resorts and retreats (Baguio, Banaue and Sagada), several active and rather threatening volcanoes (Pinatubo, Mayon, Bulusan and Taal), wildlife-watching opportunities (Donsol), and finally, of course, to the nation's capital, Manila.

Most of these places are quite accessible from Manila, and together they encapsulate Luzon's long history and hugely varied – and very active – landscape and environment, bringing together the very best that the northern half of the Philippines has to offer the traveller. There is without doubt something for everyone here, from the history and culture buff, to the surfing dude and mountain hiker, to the wildlife and nature watcher. A journey through Luzon will cover all of it.

Left: A placid lake lies surrounded by rugged and eroding rock walls; the caldera that marks ground zero for Mt Pinatubo's huge 1991 eruption, carving out this deceptively peaceful landscape.

PAGUDPUD AND THE LAOAG AREA

LUZON'S NORTHERN SHORES

The far northern coasts of Luzon are ruggedly beautiful and relatively thinly populated, with the northernmost mountains of the Cordillera Central, many of them still forested, crowding against a narrow coastal plain.

CHURCH, LAKE AND DUNES

Places of interest start just to the south of Laoag, the capital of Ilocos Norte province, in the small town of Paoay. This is the location of the Church of San Agustin, a huge 18th-century Spanish church that is now a UNESCO World Heritage Site. It was built in the 'earthquake baroque' style typical of the Spanish Philippines, meaning that it has a relatively ornate facade but was built with massive fortress-like walls intended to resist both earthquake and attack. Huge buttresses support the external walls, while inside it is pleasing in its delicate simplicity, quite the antithesis of that massive external structure.

To the north is Paoay Lake, actually a national park, but long degraded from the wildlife conservation perspective due to encroachment by farmland and villages. Nevertheless, it is a peaceful and calming place to relax and just enjoy the view.

Between here and Laoag stretches a vast expanse of coastal sand dunes, the Suba Dunes. In the area just south of Laoag, it is popular to go careering across the dunes in all terrain vehicles (ATVs), mostly following well-worn tracks. It is a very bumpy, but nevertheless exhilarating ride.

Once beyond Laoag, a relatively small and pleasant town, the road hugs the coast, with rocks, cliffs and the blue open sea constantly off to the left, and dark green, cloud-capped mountains coming in ever closer on the right. At Cape Bojeador the road passes a lighthouse, and the coast then does a sharp right turn, marking the spot where Luzon's west coast, facing the South China Sea, becomes the country's north-facing cap. This is the start of the Babuyan Channel, separating the mainland from the scattered Babuyan and Batanes Islands to the north and eventually linking through to the Pacific Ocean to the east.

THE BEACHES OF PAGUDPUD

Beyond here lies Bangui Bay, at the western end of which, along a vast shingle beach stands a curving line of huge wind turbines. Not to everyone's aesthetic taste, it has to be said, they certainly are an

enormously striking piece of modern architecture-cum-sculpture. They have also provided an unexpected boost to local tourism, the site now hosting a growing line of stalls selling quite a plethora of windmill-type memorabilia.

Another 20 km (12 miles) further brings you to the beaches of Pagudpud, the far north's main tourism attraction. Consisting of three beaches – the first two with spectacular golden sand, the third a vast expanse of grey sand and shingle – spread along 20 km (12 miles) of coast, Pagudpud has been steadily gaining in popularity.

The first of the beaches is Saud, the most well-established of the three; a truly vast beach, its fine sand stretching for several kilometres along a curving bay. The shore drops quite steeply into relatively deep water not far from the beach, but fortunately the sea here is usually rather calm – making it a good place for swimming – protected as it is from Pacific swells by Mayraira Point, the Philippine mainland's northernmost tip, just to the east.

Further east, and on the opposite side of Mayraira Point, is Pagudpud's second beach, Blue Lagoon. Reached from the main coast road via a steep, rough track, this is a stunningly beautiful place, a tightly curving bay lined by golden sand and washed by deeply blue and brilliantly white rolling waves. It is all backed by emerald green forested mountains that crowd in very close, dropping steeply down to the shore.

Above: A group of visitors heads off on the start of an all-terrain-vehicle journey across the rolling Suba Dunes, just south of Laoag city, one of the area's main visitor attractions.

Top: The calm, reflective waters of Paoay Lake, surrounded by a peaceful bucolic landscape, near the town of Paoay.

Opposite: Paoay's huge 18th-century Church of San Agustin, one of the largest and most historic relics of the Spanish era, today a UNESCO World Heritage Site.

Quite different from the vast Saud Beach, Blue Lagoon is a much more energized kind of place, its exposure to the Pacific rollers making sure of that. Indeed, it was first 'discovered' as a surfing venue, its main surf break right outside the Kapuluan Vista Resort, one of the first to be built at Blue Lagoon. The main surfing season here is during the south-west monsoon (July to September) when the wind is offshore.

Further to the east of Blue Lagoon and close to the border with Cagayan province, stretches the grey sand and shingle of Pannzian Beach (sometimes spelled Pansian). Perhaps a little disappointing after Saud and Blue Lagoon, this is nevertheless a huge beach, and one that is definitely not busy.

HEADING INLAND

Although most of Pagudpud's attractions undoubtedly lie along the coast, it is possible to make some forays inland, striking out into the northern foothills of the Cordillera Central. There are a number of fairly serious hiking and mountain-biking opportunities, but for the less energetic there is a short walk up to nearby Kabigan Falls. Lying on the very edge of the foothills, the falls are a 30-minute hike from the nearest road, initially across vibrantly green rice fields, and then through some rainforest, climbing relatively gently up the first hillside, all under the shade of a tree canopy. The waterfall itself is quite lovely, surrounded by forest trees and cascading down a sheer cliff into a pool that is a popular swimming place for both locals and visitors.

Above right: Although Blue Lagoon is now well known for its lovely beach, it was originally made popular by its excellent surfing.

Right: Pagudpud's most well-established resorts lie along the vast Saud Beach, a huge curving stretch of sand, protected from Pacific swells by Mayraira Point, the mainland's northernmost headland.

Opposite: An alternative to Pagudpud's beaches is the stunning Kabugan Falls, a few kilometres inland and on the northern edge of the foothills that rise up into the Cordillera Central mountains.

VIGAN

HISPANIC COLONIAL HERITAGE

Sitting on Luzon's north-west coast, Vigan is a relatively small town, but its importance reaches well beyond anything related to size. For it is the site of the most well-preserved Spanish colonial settlement in the Philippines, giving quite a clear illustration of what life may well have been like during Spanish rule. This is another UNESCO World Heritage Site, ensuring that the settlement's previously dilapidated buildings are steadily and sensitively being restored, bringing life to the streets and putting Vigan firmly on the tourist trail.

Not that the whole of Vigan is a preserved museum to colonial life, far from it. Most of it is much like any other Philippine town; bustling, noisy, colourful, more than just a little chaotic. However, the historic part of town, known as the Mestizo District, named after the mixed Spanish-Chinese-Filipino families who formed Spanish Philippines' wealthier class, lies at Vigan's very heart.

Above: Calle Crisologo, the heart of Vigan's Mestizo District, in the evening, complete with a *calesa*, a horse-drawn carriage, that is the only type of vehicle allowed inside the historic area.

Left: Historic Hispanic furniture creates the perfect period scene in the villa-cum-hotel of Villa Angela.

Opposite top: Sheltered by a canopy, the upstairs window of this colonial-style house consists of a traditional sliding frame 'glazed' with capiz shells.

Opposite below: A busy daytime scene on Calle Crisologo, showing off the classic Hispanic architecture of the streetside buildings.

VIGAN'S BEGINNINGS

Vigan was a busy port long before the Spanish arrived, with strong trading links not just to other centres around Southeast Asia, but also to China and the Arab world. The Spanish showed up in 1572, under the leadership of Juan de Salcedo, grandson of Miguel Lopez de Legaspi, the man who began the process of bringing the Philippines under Spanish control. Salcedo quickly established Vigan as a regional centre for Spanish government, from which point the town we see today developed.

Vigan did become one of the earliest centres for Philippine opposition to Spanish rule. Diego Silang took control of the town in 1762, maintaining his position until his assassination a couple of years later. From then on his wife, Gabriela, took over the mantle of revolutionary leader, until she was captured and then executed in Vigan's main square.

Vigan's importance as both a trading and a governmental town under the Spanish led to the growth of an aristocracy, mainly among the Mestizos, and it is largely the buildings their wealth created in the 19th century that we see today.

EXPLORING THE HISTORIC QUARTER

Ringed around Calle Crisologo, the Mestizo District's main street, the historic area consists of a grid of narrow roads and alleys from which all traffic has been banned, apart from *calesas*, small horse-drawn carriages that serve as the local taxis, sending the classic clip-clopping sound of hooves on cobbles reverberating around the district. The buildings lining the streets are mostly two-storey, designed in a classically Hispanic colonial style that is not simply Castillian, but that also shows significant Mexican, Chinese and Philippine influences. With most buildings, the ground floor is built of stone or brick covered with plaster, the upper storey a light wooden structure, with the frame broken up by large sliding windows glazed not with heavy glass but with beautifully delicate capiz shells. Taken from a flat bivalve mollusc, this was a very traditional Filipino way of 'glazing' a window, translucent rather than transparent.

Scattered around the district are several quite striking villas, a number of which are now either museums or hotels. A beautiful example of the latter is Villa Angela, a hotel in the south of the district, itself a living museum to the colonial era, filled with classically Hispanic furniture made from dark hardwood, much of it originally brought from Mexico.

But the crowning glory of the Mestizo District must be the magnificent St Paul's Cathedral, completed at the end of the 18th century. Sitting next to Vigan's two main squares, Plazas Salcedo and Burgos, at the northern end of Calle Crisologo, it is a pale yellow, plaster-covered building, the inside beautifully white-washed, both calming and refreshing to look at, and very cooling to sit in on a hot day. Standing on the site of at least two previous churches, both destroyed by earthquakes, St Paul's – like San Agustin in Paoay to the north – is built in the massive 'earthquake baroque' style.

INTO THE MODERN TOWN

The modern Vigan, starting beyond the cathedral, is of course a colourful, crowded place, its streets filled with noisy jeepneys and tricycles, just the occasional clip-clop of a *calesa* breaking in. But it is a town to which historic fame has brought relative wealth, and an air of confidence and civic pride. Many of the main streets are tree-lined, the plazas and parks are well cared-for, and the crazy musical fountains in Plaza Salcedo, played each evening in the summer months, are just a joy to watch!

At the southern end of town the noise fades away again in a series of tree-lined boulevards that lead to two more of Vigan's points of interest: in the south-west a cluster of potteries that make *burnay* jars, enormous pots traditionally used for storage; and in the south-east a number of weavers renowned for using locally produced natural fibres to produce traditional *barong* shirts, tablecloths and napkins. Together, they constitute an important continuation of traditional skills that very much support Vigan's great historical heritage status.

Above: A craftsman at work, incising a traditional design into a newly made *burnay* jar, before firing.

Top: The facade of the lovely 18th-century St Paul's Cathedral, one of Vigan's most historic buildings.

Opposite top: The dining room, complete with historic furniture, of Syquia Mansion, one of the city's most famous mansion museums.

Opposite below: In Vigan even the humble tricycle reflects history in the intricate decorations of their highly polished, metallic canopies.

SAN JUAN, LA UNION

A WEST COAST SURF MECCA

It may be true that the Philippines' Pacific, east coast catches most of the glory as the focus for the country's greatest surfing venues, but even the quieter, more sheltered west coast can catch a few good waves in places. Some of the best of that west coast surf comes ashore on a long, sandy beach close to the unassuming village of San Juan, in north-west Luzon, just a few hours' drive from Manila.

Barely even marked on the maps in the late 1990s, today San Juan is rated as one of the Philippines' main surfing centres, its accessibility from the capital certainly a major factor. Sitting on La Union's coast just a few kilometres north of the port city of San Fernando, right beside northern Luzon's main north-south highway, San Juan could hardly be easier to find.

The resorts that have sprung up along the shore here exist for surfing, the sport radically boosting the local economy over the past few years, giving some of the local kids a whole new, and unexpected, career. While most make a living from teaching visitors how to surf, a few are now among the country's top surfers, able to compete on the international circuit.

THE SAN JUAN SCENE

The San Juan beach runs for several magnificent kilometres almost directly north-south, in places barely a couple of hundred metres from the main highway. The 'downtown' part of the village sprawls along the highway, roughly coinciding with the beach's mid-section, but unfortunately with its back turned towards the sea – until recently the beach held little interest for the local people.

The sand here is not of the blinding white variety that so typifies the coral sand beaches of the Visayas further south. Instead, it is generally a rather dark yellow-brown sort of hue, which turns more golden during the driest summer months of April and May. The sand is, however, mostly quite fine and soft, so apart from the less-than-perfect colour, it is a great beach. And anyway, most visitors' attention is focussed on the water, and how those rolling waves are performing as they rush up towards the beach.

Those waves do not perform all year. San Juan's surfing season runs from October to March, during the north-east monsoon, a time when the winds coming in across the Pacific send a strong swell around the northern tip of Luzon and down its west coast, the resultant waves coming ashore at places like San Juan. During the rest of the year, when ironically the winds are onshore, the seas are mostly too calm to produce the necessary waves. At this time, San Juan is a good place just for swimming and paddle-boarding, and for the really little ones – the surfer dudes of the future – to use the miniature waves to develop their skills.

Left: Although much of San Juan's beach is open sand, at its main centre gazebos mark the sites of a series of surfing schools. San Juan is one of the Philippines' main hotspots for learning the sport.

Right: An early evening view of the southern end of the San Juan beach at Urbiztondo.

SURFING ACTION AT URBIZTONDO

Most of the action is concentrated at the southernmost end, in San Juan's Urbiztondo *barangay*, where the beach curves into a small bay that separates it from the rest of the north-south beach. To the south, the beach ends in a small headland of coralline rock, a wonderful vantage point from which to watch the surfing side-on to the action, and in the evening to watch the sun very atmospherically dip below the horizon across the South China Sea.

A few fishermen still operate with their boats and nets from this bay, but mostly this strip of sand is now lined with resorts and hostels, a slightly jumbled clutter of buildings that is slowly moving upmarket as the surfing scene attracts more visitors and finance. Behind the resorts, the main highway is lined with a steadily expanding number of bars and restaurants, that slowly but surely are turning this into a semi-urban nightspot.

Much of the best surf comes ashore in this bay, and it is here that most of the surfing schools and instructors congregate to teach an ever-growing band of people eager to learn the art of riding the waves. The biggest waves, however, come ashore at Mona Liza Point, a spit of sand that marks the northern end of Urbiztondo's curving bay, where it joins up with the main north-south stretch of sand. It is here that most of San Juan's popular surfing contests are held.

North of Mona Liza Point the beach remains largely empty and undeveloped for several kilometres, used only by a few fishermen and walkers. This is probably due to the steeply shelving nature of the sand along this stretch, making it less attractive, and indeed more dangerous, for both surfers and swimmers than the gently sloping Urbiztondo bay. Continuing yet further north, to the Montemar *barangay*, the sand once again slopes more gently, and here several more resorts have been developed, complete with surfing instructors.

These pages: Surfing is the name of the game at San Juan, even in calm weather, a time that is ideal for novices. A new surfer learns to hitch a ride on a modest bit of surf (top). An old hand takes to jumping on a skim board to ride into the oncoming waves (left). Shortly before sunset, beginners practise new-found skills in the smaller waves (above). Surfing wannabes get an early morning lesson (opposite).

BEYOND THE SURF

For those who tire of the beach and its surf, there is always nearby San Fernando. A small port city, it has a lively, bustling and colourful street life, particularly in the streets around the market, where stalls sell everything from vegetables to pots and pans, to satay chicken with coconut milk.

To the west of the city centre and port lies Poro Point, once upon a time an American base, but now redeveloped as a tourism and commercial zone, complete with the grandly named Thunderbird Poro Point Hotel, site of a casino and a sprawling golf course.

East of the city centre, and roughly on the way back towards San Juan, is San Fernando's most important cultural site: the Ma-Cho Temple, a Chinese Taoist temple. Although the Philippines is of course overwhelmingly a Catholic Christian country, the Chinese have always had a significant commercial presence, particularly in the cities. The occasional manifestation of this is a Chinese temple, and San Fernando's Ma-cho is one of the nicest.

The temple is dedicated to Mazu, Goddess of the Sea and protectress of fishermen, a divinity that originated as a real historical figure in China's south-eastern Fujian province. Over the centuries she has become of huge importance to coastal Chinese communities everywhere.

It is rather a steep climb up to the temple, but it is worth the effort, not only for the fun and liveliness of its colourful, sweeping, dragon-topped eaves and gateways, but also for the sense of peace and thoughtfulness that pervades the site, overhung with dense vegetation, the aroma of incense wafting through the air. It is quite the antidote to the busy streets below!

It also represents a very different world view from that of the surfer scene, but who knows: perhaps as Goddess of the Sea, Mazu would smile on the brash new generation of surfers, riding the waves and boosting the local economy just a short distance to the north.

Opposite page: San Fernando's colourful, bustling market is a place to be explored and enjoyed, its traders selling a huge wealth of products, from locally grown vegetables to dried fish and garden plants.

Right: The main gateway to the Chinese Taoist Ma-Cho Temple, topped by the protective powers of writhing dragons underneath which is the Taoist octagon, the *bagua*, containing the eight trigrams of Taoism.

Below: The main shrine of San Fernando's Ma-Cho Temple, housing (behind the glass) an effigy of Mazu, Goddess of the Sea and protectress of fishermen.

HUNDRED ISLANDS NATIONAL PARK

A BIJOU ARCHIPELAGO

Actually 123 islands to be exact, the Hundred Islands National Park is a lovely mini-archipelago, a tight cluster of vibrantly green islands and islets lying in a bright azure sea, a very scenic part of the Lingayen Gulf, itself a sweeping indented bay on the west coast of northern Luzon.

The roughly 18 sq km (seven square miles) that the national park covers is basically the fragmented remains of a vast raised coral reef, eroded by the sea into some strange shapes, most of the islands little more than rough coralline limestone outcrops capped by a tangle of vegetation, and with nowhere to land. A few of the larger islands do, however, have small beaches where landing is possible, and from there you can often explore strange rock formations and caves, as well as get great views of the islands, and of course do some swimming and snorkelling off the beach.

ISLAND HOPPING

These islands are very popular – perhaps a little too popular, especially at weekends – as a place to motor around in boats or fool about in the sand. The start and finish point for everyone is the harbour at Lucap, a fishing village on the mainland coast, just on the edge of the town of Alaminos. Here, a fleet of *bancas* waits to be hired for tours out to and around the islands. Although Lucap harbour is not an especially pleasant place – it was hugely expanded in what looks like quite a hurry a few years ago – it works well, the harbour managers ensuring an efficient (and fixed-price) boat-hiring process.

It is a 15-minute trip out across the sheltered bay to the waters of the even more sheltered archipelago, and once among the islands you are surrounded by mirror-calm turquoise water, the deeply, irridescently green islands crowding in around. Most of the islands are ringed by some very jagged-looking, boat-unfriendly rocks and cliffs, many of the latter undercut by the waves. As a result, some of the islands seriously overhang the bases of their cliffs, looking as though they might be undermined and so collapse at any minute. In fact, a number look as though that is exactly what has happened to them.

Not surprisingly, the boat crews know exactly which islands can be landed on, and they are only too keen to make sure you get to them. Only three have any development: Children's, Governor's and Quezon Islands. Apart from these three, several more islands are worth exploring, including Marcos Island, site of a beautiful sea cave. Swimmers frequently dive into the blue-green water inside the cave and then swim out under the low rock arch that separates the cave from the sea, and back to the nearby beach.

All three of the developed islands have small beaches, those on Children's Island particularly sheltered and child-friendly. Governor's Island has a little taste of island hiking on offer, paths leading through the dense tangled scrub, principally to a viewpoint at the top of a particularly rocky outcrop, with stupendous views across the islands.

Quezon Island is almost certainly the most popular of the islands among local visitors. One of the islands furthest from the mainland, it has probably the national park's largest and best beach, reaching from Quezon itself across to an adjoining islet. Here there is a giant clam-breeding centre, set up to restore the decimated population of what was once an iconic species of these islands. The wooded slopes of both islands have a liberal scattering of picnic and barbecue sites, complete with sheltered seats, some overhanging the low cliffs and with great views out across the beach. A wooden walkway has also been built out from Quezon across to another nearby, previously inaccessible islet, perhaps rather marring the natural beauty of the seascape, but greatly expanding the possibilities for walking around and generally exploring.

Above: Most of the Hundred Islands' islets consist of little more than scrub-covered, coralline limestone rock outcrops. The sea's undermining action creates overhangs just above the waves, leaving nowhere to land.

Left: Fishermen unloading their catch at Lucap harbour: a couple of small sharks.

Opposite: The view inside Imelda Cave, a popular swimming hole, with access to the sea beyond, on Marcos Island.

THE NATURAL ENVIRONMENT

The national park has been under huge environmental pressure for years, both its fish stocks and coral reefs decimated by dynamite fishing long before it became popular with visitors. There is some hope that this may be improving now, not only with the giant clam-breeding site, but also due to fishing patrols put in place by the local government. In recent years, there have been reports of Dugong, dolphins and several species of turtle being found among the islands.

Not surprisingly with such a small group of islands, terrestrial wildlife is rather limited, though Long-tailed Macaques, civets, Monitor Lizards and several bat species are known to live here. Over 100 species of bird have been recorded in the islands, both marine and woodland birds, some resident others just passing through during seasonal migrations. Those on the list include reef egrets and Purple Herons, plus several species each of kingfisher, pigeon and flowerpecker, to name just the most well known.

Above left: A view of the Hundred Islands archipelago from the viewpoint on Governor's Island.

Above right: Sunset over some of the outermost islands, seen from Quezon Island.

Right: The beach on Quezon Island is without doubt the national park's most popular.

BAGUIO

CAPITAL OF THE CORDILLERA

It is a relatively short drive from the coastal plains around the lowland towns of Rosario and Agoo, in La Union province, up to the mountain city of Baguio, but the steep climb that the journey entails transports you to a wholly different environment. As the road twists and turns its way up the mountainsides, so you leave behind the rice fields and palm trees, and arrive in a world of vegetable plots and pine forests. You have left the tropics and entered a temperate world. Welcome to the Cordillera Central, the rugged, mountainous spine that covers much of northern Luzon.

Right: Close-up of the front of a colourful jeepney, the ubiquitous Filipino minibus that clogs Baguio's streets.

Opposite: The main restaurant in the Manor, one of Baguio's most exclusive hotels and at the heart of Camp John Hay.

Below: The extremely popular boating lake in Burnham Park, in the centre of Baguio.

THE MOUNTAIN CITY

The first stop for almost everyone taking that road is Baguio, administrative capital of Benguet province, and both commercial centre and transport hub for the whole of the Cordillera. For foreign visitors from cooler climates, Baguio represents a respite from the heat and humidity of lowland Philippines. For Filipinos, it is a chance to experience a quite different climate without having to leave the country, though many find the Cordillera actually a little too cold, particularly at night. At an altitude of 1,450 metres (4,756 ft), it is the Philippines' only temperate, highland city.

Many first-time visitors can be a little disappointed to find that Baguio is not some quiet mountain retreat far removed from the lowland crowds. With a population of just over 300,000, it is a major city, by far the largest in the Cordillera. And just like every other Philippine city, its streets are clogged with revving, smoke-belching jeepneys that sadly have given the city centre an unenviable reputation for air pollution.

CAMP JOHN HAY

Fortunately, there is a lot more to Baguio, for out to the east, and occupying a far larger area than the city centre, are rolling, park-like, pine-clad hills, mostly enclosed within Camp John Hay. Formerly an American military camp, this is now a mix of forest, parkland, a magnificent golf course, small shopping centres and restaurants, and site of The Manor, one of the city's most beautiful and most upmarket hotels. The entire Camp is still enclosed, gated and guarded, ensuring that it retains an air of exclusivity. The fact that jeepneys are banned is a further benefit, keeping traffic levels low and the air clean, the scent of the pine trees quite clearly detectable.

Beyond the Camp's northern edge, the landscape remains largely green and pine-clad. This is the site of some of Baguio's attractions, including the Botanic Garden, Wright Park, The Mansion and Mines View Park. The Botanic Garden, though not in the same league as some of Southeast Asia's world-class botanic gardens, is nevertheless

a lovely, lushly vegetated park, complete with a number of reconstructions of traditional houses of the Ifugao, one of the main minority tribes that lives in the Cordillera. The nearby Wright Park has – it has to be admitted – seen better days, but it is a popular place, at least in part because it is one of the very few places where anyone can hire a pony and ride around a little. You cannot ride very far, and the ponies look a little strange, their manes dyed all sorts of lurid colours for reasons best known to their owners, but it all looks harmless enough!

To the south-east stands The Mansion, officially the summer residence of the Philippine president. A legacy of the days, long lost, when Baguio was the summer capital of the Philippines, The Mansion's white-washed, neo-colonial architecture, neatly clipped lawns and stiff guards retain a presidential air, though I'm not sure the president visits all that often.

Away on the eastern edge stands Mines View Park, so named after the view it has across a huge valley in which are dotted a number of

gold and copper mines. In actual fact, the mines are barely visible, and the viewpoint is far better known for its wonderful panorama across the rugged Cordillera mountains, a great sight early and late in the day. For those who like this kind of thing, it is also a great souvenir-hunting kind of place, the huge mass of souvenir stalls that crowd around the entrance to the park, making the park seem almost secondary.

That said, a better place to visit to find good-quality handicrafts would be the Easter School of Weaving, over on the western side of the city. Here, huge amounts of textiles, woven on site to patterns traditional to the people of the Cordillera, are on sale. Next door, it is possible to watch the weavers at work, using traditional hand looms to produce all those beautiful, intricate and brightly colourful fabrics.

Above: A photographer in Mines View Park provides visitors with the opportunity to dress up in the traditional clothing of the mountain region's tribal minorities. and be immortalized.

Right: Some of Baguio's best handicrafts are produced at the Easter School of Weaving, where skilled weavers produce cloth with traditional mountain patterns.

Opposite above: The lush greens of the Botanic Garden, set among pine trees.

Opposite below: Beautiful white lotus flowers in the pond at the Bell Church, a Chinese Taoist temple.

AROUND THE CITY

Despite ruling the Philippines for 350 years, the Spanish had only a relatively modest impact on the landscape and peoples of the Cordillera, and for this reason you would be hard-pressed to find much colonial Spanish influence in Baguio – unlike Luzon's lowlands you won't find any historic Spanish churches here, for example. Indeed, when the Americans took over the Philippines at the very end of the 19th century, what is now Baguio was at the time no more than an Ifugao village named Kafagway.

The new American government, however, moved quickly to establish it as their summer capital. Urban architect Daniel Burnham was brought in to design the new city, and – despite the destruction wrought by the Second World War and a huge earthquake in 1990 – the grid of streets he created is still very much at the heart of today's city centre, complete with Burnham Park and its extremely popular boating lake.

Session Road is the focus of the central shopping centre, linking at its top, uphill end, the huge, relatively modern cathedral, with the city's market at the bottom of the hill. The market is really the place to get a feel for the wealth of produce this region can grow, ranging from tropical papayas and pineapples from the lower areas, to the potatoes, cabbages and carrots of the real highland regions. The star attraction, however, for which Baguio is famous across the Philippines, is strawberries. The hills around Baguio produce masses of them, and in the market they seem to be piled high.

Better still, heading to Baguio's northern suburbs brings you to strawberry farms where it is possible for visitors to pick their own, something that is in danger of becoming just a bit too popular, with entire bus loads of visitors descending on the farms.

Not far from here are a couple more of Baguio's attractions, including Tam-Awan, a re-creation of a typical Ifugao village, with traditional houses and farm plots built across a steep hillside, affording great views across parts of the city. To the east is the Bell Church, a curious

name for what is actually a Chinese Taoist temple. As with its equivalent down in San Fernando, the temple is testament to the importance of the local Chinese community. It is a wonderful spot, complete with pagodas, sweeping eaves, ponds filled with delicate lotus flowers and enormous koi carp, and lots of vibrant red paint and green tiles, a truly colourful assault on the senses.

Baguio is quite unique in the Philippines, with its cool, temperate climate and its mountain culture, but it is still a crowded, noisy city, hardly representative of the Cordillera as a whole. To find that you need to head out into the countryside, right into the heart of the mountains, taking the Halsema Highway northwards towards Bontoc and the mountain village of Sagada.

Opposite below left: Picking strawberries at a farm on the outskirts of Baguio.

Opposite below right: A market stall loaded with a wealth of locally produced vegetables.

Opposite above: Baguio's early 20th-century cathedral dominates the uphill end of Session Road.

This page: Baguio's Chinese Taoist temple. Pavilions and ornate tiles typify the Bell Church (top). A statue of Guanyin, a Chinese Buddhist goddess, ubiquitous across Chinese temples (right).

SAGADA

A PERFECT MOUNTAIN HIDEAWAY

Lying about 230 km (143 miles) north of Baguio, tucked away in a hidden valley and surrounded by karst limestone hills and forests of pine, Sagada is one of the Cordillera's gems, a really ideal mountain retreat.

The village is reached from Baguio via the Halsema Highway, a twisting, turning, rising, falling mountain road that is arguably the most spectacular in the Philippines. Until a few years ago the Halsema was just a rough dirt road, washed out by landslides every time it rained, and a strenuous ride even at the best of times. Now it is paved all the way to its destination in Bontoc, making the trip much faster and smoother, but it is still an exhilarating road.

DRIVING THE HALSEMA HIGHWAY

The mountain views radiate all around, first on one side of the road, then on the other, at dawn the mountains little more than blue-grey outlines against a pink sky, the valley floors lost in either uncertain mist or seas of puffy, whispy clouds far below. Once the sun is up, the mist starts to dissipate, and then the mountain outlines resolve into green pine forests alternating with terraced farm fields, at this altitude producing not rice but temperate climate vegetables, such as potatoes, carrots and onions.

Villages and market towns lie dotted along the road, the latter bustling with farmers and farm produce, all set against a stunning mountain backdrop. At 2,256 metres (7,400 ft) above sea level, the road reaches its highest point – indeed the highest point on the entire Philippine road network – and here there is a viewpoint that has one of the most amazing views in the whole of the country. Looking out across an enormous valley, the view takes in much of the Cordillera Central range to the east, including the summit of Mt Pulag, at 2,930 metres (9,610 ft) Luzon's highest mountain, third highest in the country.

Shortly after here the road plunges downwards again, briefly returning to the tropics, then, after turning off the main road as it heads onwards to Bontoc, the capital of Mountain province, it climbs steeply back upwards into the hills. Once over some kind of lip the road enters a hidden valley. Occasional houses start to appear among the pines and limestone outcrops, and within a few minutes the village of Sagada appears, strung out along a narrow valley, parts of it clinging to steep slopes, all of it surrounded by mist-shrouded, pine forest-covered hills.

These pages: The mountainous landscape along the Halsema Highway is a verdant mix of dense forests of Benguet pine and terraced farm fields producing such crops as potatoes, carrots and onions.

THE SAGADA SCENE

It takes only a few minutes to realise that there is something quite different about Sagada. The air is fresh and clear, scented with nose-tingling pine, and there is a peace that is rare in the modern world. The stress and dust of the road immediately start to fall away, body and mind relax, and there then comes this overwhelming desire to do absolutely nothing – just sit and breathe the clear air and enjoy the lovely, calm view. This is the ultimate therapy.

There are, however, things for the visitor to do. The local people belong to the Applai tribe, a traditionally animist group who bury their dead in caves, of which there are many around Sagada, or even attached to cliff faces. As a result, most of the attractions revolve around visiting a few of the nearest caves and cliffs, as well as hiking along some of the many paths that criss-cross the surrounding hills and forests.

The nearest site to the centre of Sagada is Echo Valley, a deep, forested limestone gorge just off to one side of the village. Here a cluster of coffins attached to a cliff face can be seen at close quarters, many of them quite old, others put in place in just the past few years.

A couple of kilometres south of the village is Lumiang Cave, where hundreds of coffins, some thought to be as much as 500 years old, are piled up in the cave entrance. Beyond this lies Sumaguing Cave, not renowned for coffins for there are none here, but for its stunning stalactites and stalagmites. Although the cave entrance has quite a number, the best displays are deep inside, reachable only with the help of a guide and lights. Reliable guides are easily hired in the village – Sagada has been attracting a steady trickle of intrepid travellers for a long time and so guiding is well established – and they frequently lead people through this and other local caves. There are also some great hiking routes through the forests and up some of the nearby mountains, but a guide must always be hired.

If all this sounds too energetic, don't worry. Sagada is a place to relax and unwind. If lots of walking does that for you then that's great. But for those who like to just sit and watch the view, perhaps with a good drink in hand, then Sagada is the place to be.

Top left: The entire Philippine road network reaches its highest point on the Halsema Highway, a spot with some magnificent views.

Top right: A group of visitors takes a breather just outside the entrance to Sumaguing Cave.

Above: Stalactites crowd the ceiling in one of the most accessible parts of Sumaguing Cave.

Opposite: Sagada nestles in a narrow valley; steep, pine-clad hillsides crowding in all around.

BANAUE

WORLD HERITAGE RICE TERRACES

Apart from the lovely mountain scenery that surrounds it, the little town of Banaue would be rather unremarkable were it not for one thing: it is the focal point for some stupendous mountainside rice terraces that make up much of the area's agricultural landscape.

Carved out of the precipitous mountain slopes about 2,000 years ago by the direct ancestors of today's farmers, the Banaue rice terraces were awarded World Heritage Site status by UNESCO in 1995 for their huge cultural importance. If nothing else, they speak volumes about the ingenuity of those ancient farmers, at least when it comes to their skills in agricultural engineering and hydrology. Then as now, the terraces were farmed for rice by members of the Ifugao community, a tribe, or cultural minority, that make up much of the population across this region of the Cordillera Central mountains.

EXPLORING THE RICE TERRACES

Banaue itself is a slightly untidy town, clinging to the slopes of a steep mountainside in a deep valley, sitting beside the main road from Manila to Bontoc, and surrounded by mixed agricultural and forest land. There are a few rice terraces immediately around the town, though generally rather small, gentle affairs.

A couple of kilometres uphill above Banaue, along the main road, is a viewpoint that looks out over the town's nearest set of large steep terraces. Being right next to the main road, it is here that many visitors come, and so not surprisingly the viewpoint is surrounded by a sprawling mass of stalls selling souvenirs and snacks, while a group of increasingly senior Ifugao citizens dressed in traditional clothes pose for the photographers, in return for a small tip.

It is rather unfortunate that this very accessible set of rice terraces is no longer quite what it was, in recent years a number of them having been abandoned by the latest generation in favour of a less arduous urban life.

To see the *real* rice terraces you need to head away from Banaue into remoter parts, where the fields are still fully cultivated. Two such areas are relatively accessible from Banaue, the nearest down into a valley at a lower altitude and around the villages of Hapao and Hungduan, easily reached by vehicle. The second, around the village of Batad, requires rather more effort to get to as some hiking is involved, but the reward is really worthwhile.

HUNGDUAN AND HAPAO

Whereas in the lowlands rice cultivation can be almost a continuous cycle, here in the mountains it is controlled not just by the rainy season but also by temperature, and specifically the arrival of warmer springtime temperatures. As in any other mountainous country, cultivation starts later the higher up you climb. Hapao and Hungduan are among the lowest areas of this rice-growing region, so rice cultivation starts here first, the terraces turning an irridescent green with young rice plants by March.

Both villages lie down in a steep valley, reached via a minor road turning off the main one north of Banaue. Initially, the sides of the valley are very steep and there is not a lot of cultivation. However, as the road dips so the valley opens out into a relatively gently sloping bowl, and it is here that the rice terraces are concentrated, looking more like gentle steps, wide and with a small gradient, giving the valley's lower slopes and floor a carpet of green.

At Hapao there is also a small museum mostly outdoors and spreading across a hillside, dedicated to showing off the traditional life of the Ifugao people. Several traditional Ifugao houses are on show here, along with a number of household utensils and farming tools.

These pages: The rice terraces of Hungduan and Hapao, vibrantly green in April, are on a relatively gentle hillside, fanning out into broad fields in the valley floor, each one reachable along a network of narrow paths.

BATAD

Several hundred metres higher up the mountains than Hapao and Hungduan, Batad is a much colder place, and rice cultivation starts here at least a month later. So, at a time when the fields of the lower villages are carpeted with green, around Batad the farmers are only just starting to transplant their delicate rice seedlings.

To get there, a hired jeepney can take you some way up into the mountains above Banaue, but eventually you will reach track's end in a clearing close to a ridge. From here, the footpath to Batad leads over the ridge, and then steeply downhill and eventually into the village. There are stunning views across a huge amphitheatre-like valley, completely hemmed in by steep mountains. All around, rice terraces cling to precipitous slopes, starting at the very floor of the valley and climbing one on top of the other to the heights above. Here and there, on the less steep slopes, sits the occasional farm or hamlet, many still containing traditional Ifugao houses, although generally, alas, with the thatched roof replaced by corrugated metal.

It is quite a spectacle, and one that just has to be explored. The farmers' paths along the terrace edges naturally make for some great routes along which to hike up and down the valley slopes. Just take care about where you put your feet – the paths are usually quite narrow, and the drop down to the terrace immediately below quite significant!

These pages: Around Batad, the rice terraces cling to steep mountainsides, forming a natural amphitheatre. Hamlets are clustered tightly on vantage points among the terraces.

BEYOND THE SURF

For those not attempting to ride the waves there is plenty of exploring to be done. To the south of Sabang beach the sand comes to an abrupt halt at the mouth of Tibag River, flowing down from the nearby mountains. Small fishing communities lie on both sides of the estuary, the local children already honing their surfing skills using small homemade boards on the surf that builds up in the river mouth. Inside the estuary, the river's banks are worth exploring for its mangrove and nipa palm forests, and the river itself can be crossed on a long cable suspension footbridge, the best spot for clear views up and down the river.

Continuing south along the coast, a rough road both becomes a gateway to the area's largely untouched tropical rainforests, and leads to some stunning coastal viewpoints and hidden coves. Apart from views of blue and white Pacific surf pounding the sheer cliffs, head and shoulders above all is the stunning Dicasalarin Cove, a pristine arc of blindingly white sand, hemmed in by mountains and emerald green rainforest, lying at road's end about 10 km (six miles) south of Baler. Anyone wanting to really get away from everything could stay here – there are a few simple bungalows, owned by the Costa Pacifica. The trees crowd in all around, so it would almost certainly be possible to organize hiking trips from here out into some pristine rainforest.

Continuing the theme of Baler as gateway to the forests, for the adventurous the town can be used as a starting point for trips up into the very remote and mountainous forest areas to the north, the start of the vast and hugely important protected areas that lie along the Pacific coast and the spine of the Northern Sierra Madre.

Above: The stunningly beautiful, and very remote, Dicasalarin Cove, to the south of Baler, fronted by Pacific surf, backed by rainforest-clad mountains.

Left: A *banca* motors out through the surf at the mouth of Tibag River, on the southern edge of Baler.

Opposite top: A dense nipa palm swamp crowds in along the edge of a side-creek off the Tibag River.

Opposite below: A suspension bridge stretches out across the Tibag River, linking a fishing village on the south bank with Baler town on the north.

DITUMABO FALLS

For those just in search of a taste of the Sierra Madre forests there's Ditumabo Falls, or Mother Falls, about 10 km (six miles) inland from Baler. The waterfall is reached via a short drive from the main road up a rough track, followed by a 30-minute hike along a path through farmland, scrub and rainforest. For most of its way the path follows a babbling brook, heavily overhung by trees and bamboo, on several occasions fording the river across submerged and slippery rocks. Eventually, the path passes through a small gorge and then finishes in a cliff-lined bowl down the far side of which cascades a vertical ribbon of water. The water crashes into an inviting pool, often filled with swimmers, the impact of waterfall on pool sending out a perpetual mist of refreshing spray.

It always seems a bit of a cliché to describe a place as a hidden gem, but in Baler's case it seems to be a highly apt description. It is certainly hidden – the Sierra Madre Mountains and the Pacific Ocean see to that. And in the unspoiled impact of its vast natural beauty it is quite definitely a gem. Long may it remain so!

These pages: The water in the lovely Ditumabo Falls cascades down a lushly vegetated cliff into an inviting pool, which is then drained by a rock-strewn brook.

MT PINATUBO

A VOLCANO EXPEDITION

The date 15 June 1991 is scorched indelibly into modern Philippine history, as it was on this day that the hitherto little-known Mt Pinatubo exploded in a cataclysmic volcanic eruption that devastated large swathes of northern Luzon, and that continues to have repercussions to this day.

The second largest eruption experienced by the entire world throughout the 20th century, all the numbers associated with the Pinatubo eruption are staggering. The exploding column of ash was fired nearly 40 km (25 miles) upwards, carrying with it an estimated 10 cubic km (2½ cubic miles) of debris and 20 million tonnes of sulphur dioxide. Much of this travelled several times around the globe in the upper atmosphere, reducing global temperatures by an average of 0.5°C (0.9°F) for the next two years, and damaging the Earth's ozone layer.

LIFE UNDER THE ERUPTION

For the hundreds of thousands of people living around the volcano those numbers were academic, as their homes were crushed under a deluge of ash that turned day into night as far away as Manila (90 km/56 miles south-east). The horror story was made worse by the simultaneous arrival of Typhoon Yunya, whose rains turned the ash into torrents of lahar, or volcanic mud, which tore down Pinatubo's slopes, burying towns and villages, changing forever the landscape for miles around.

Fortunately, both Philippine and US volcanologists had seen the eruption coming, and managed to persuade much of the population to evacuate, saving thousands of lives. Even so, the lahar flows took their toll, resulting in an official death toll of 847.

THE AFTERMATH

The lahar and ash created a lunar landscape, with deposits around Pinatubo estimated to be up to 200 m (656 ft) deep. Not only were settlements and farmland buried, but forests were destroyed, rivers dammed and rerouted. For years afterwards, any rains resulted in landslides and flooding as the fragile lahar deposits collapsed and reformed under the rainfall. This continues to be a threat to this day.

On Pinatubo itself, its original mountain summit, at 1,745 m (5,741 ft), was blasted away, replaced by a crater, or caldera, 2.5 km (1½ miles) across and filled with a blue-green lake, the highest point of the surrounding caldera walls at just 1,485 m (4,886 ft).

EXPLORING TODAY'S PINATUBO

More than a quarter of a century on and things seem to be relatively quiet around Pinatubo, allowing the mystique of that mighty eruption to start to become a tourism draw. However, although the volcano may be returning to the slumber that, prior to 1991, had lasted for 500 years, the landscape around it remains fragile and potentially dangerous, putting a tight limitation on just how much tourism there can be.

Today, the caldera lake is accessible, with the main starting point from the village of Sta Juliana, on Pinatubo's northern side, and from where a 4x4 route follows the Crow Valley up onto the mountain's slopes. There are, however, strict controls. For starters, the mountain is only open during the dry season, from November to May: the lahar landscape is far too fragile to risk entering during the rains. What is more, all trips must use a local 4x4 vehicle and driver plus a local guide, and they must start before 8am and finish by mid-afternoon, to avoid the risk of being caught in an afternoon shower.

It all sounds very much like an expedition out into the wilderness, but the guides and drivers have become so well practised that it all feels perfectly safe and almost effortless. Just exactly what the trip consists of varies from year to year, depending on how much the preceding rainy

season's downpours have remodelled the landscape. However, essentially, it consists of a one-hour drive across a desolate lunar landscape, the track criss-crossing meandering streams and rivers, increasingly tall and weirdly shaped pinnacles of grey rock and lahar closing in as the valley narrows.

Eventually, the 4x4 track comes to an end, and from here it is another 90-minute hike uphill through a rugged valley, again criss-crossing a stream. For much of the way, the ground is bare rock and ash, here and there streaked with minerals, mostly the oranges of iron. At a few sites the charred remains of pre-eruption forests can be seen protruding through gouged-out valley walls, most clearly still buried beneath tens of metres of lahar. In the final couple of kilometres, as the path climbs higher, so it starts to enter some vegetation, initially grasses but then the occasional tree fern and clusters of small, gnarled trees.

Eventually, the path bursts out onto a viewpoint above the caldera lake, a spectacular view across calm, shimmering water, all of it surrounded by almost sheer, and visibly steadily collapsing cliffs. A steep, stepped path leads down to a gravelly shore, though the area that can be explored is very limited, the site hemmed in by cliffs and jagged peaks. It doesn't take long to run out of angles and viewpoints to explore, and once you've finished gazing upon the lake, there is nothing left to do but start the return journey.

You've had your glimpse of the mighty Pinatubo.

Opposite: The journey up Pinatubo starts with a 4x4 drive through a rugged lunar landscape, criss-crossing streams in the walled-in valley.

Above: It ends with a hike that, on its upper slopes, passes through scrub consisting of small trees, tall grasses and the occasional tree fern.

Next page: The destination consists of a viewpoint and a beach with a vista across a vast caldera lake, surrounded by dramatic and eroding volcanic slopes.

METRO MANILA

THE NATION'S CAPITAL

A vast, crowded metropolis, home to roughly 20 per cent of the Philippines' population, it has to be admitted that Metro Manila is not the most beautiful place in the world, but it certainly is colourful and vibrant; not only the nation's capital but also its economic and cultural beating heart. With most of the Philippines' big business, financial and cultural activities focussed in and around Metro Manila, much of what defines the modern country emanates from this urban sprawl, so it is no wonder that Filipinos are drawn to it in the hope of making their mark and achieving success.

CITIES WITHIN THE CITY

For the visitor, this can be a bewildering city. For one thing, there is not one single central area but several, the result of this being a fusion of a number of cities, long ago swallowed up in the metropolis – hence the title of 'Metro'. Manila itself was the original capital, and is still one of Metro Manila's major hubs alongside the other cities that make up Metro Manila: principally Pasay to the south, Quezon City to the north-east, and Makati and Pasig City to the east. Each city has a slightly different atmosphere: Manila, for example, is the historic heart that attracts most visitor attention, Quezon is home to many of the government buildings and Makati is the centre of much of the city's modern business and commercial activity, the place where you'll find most of the skyscrapers, lined up along wide, neatly laid-out boulevards. The latest addition to the modern face of the metropolis is Bonifacio Global City, a total redevelopment of previously military land into a zone of glittering tower blocks, site of a string of corporate head offices, as well as bars and restaurants.

Most of Metro Manila, particularly some of the older areas, can be very crowded, even frenetic at times. The resulting dense traffic can make it difficult to get around, a problem not helped by the fact that the public transport network is not as logical or as well developed as perhaps it could be. Fortunately – and this is a major boon for visitors – there are vast numbers of taxis, whose drivers are expert at cutting through the heaving streets.

INTRAMUROS: MANILA'S HISTORIC HEART

Much of what is of interest to the visitor lies in and around the historic parts of Manila, particularly a collection of some wonderful museums, all of which are really worth exploring. The starting point is Intramuros, the old Spanish walled city that sits on the southern shore of the mouth of the Pasig River. Dating from the 16th century, this was the original Spanish colonial capital, built on the site of the previous town of Maynilad. Today, the huge stone fortifications stand as strong and resilient as ever, though little of the old town inside remains, most of it destroyed during fighting towards the end of the Second World War.

The one historic building to have come through it all is the 16th century San Agustin Church, the oldest in the Philippines. Little more than a few imposing walls pierced by a doorway when seen from the outside, inside it is a spectacular church, with adjacent tropical cloisters and a museum housing priceless artefacts dating from the earliest days of Spanish rule. Perhaps a little surprisingly, this is not the centre of Catholicism in the Philippines. That honour belongs to Manila Cathedral, a 1950s reconstruction that replaced the historic cathedral destroyed in the war, and which stands just a short distance down the road.

Directly across the road from San Agustin Church stands Casa Manila, a recreation of an Hispanic villa now containing a museum to the domestic life of the colonial elite. Much of the museum consists of reconstructed villa rooms, furnished with original period pieces. It is a fascinating insight into that era of the Philippines' history.

At the northernmost tip of Intramuros stands Fort Santiago, today a memorial to José Rizal, the national hero whose writings helped to inspire the anti-Spanish revolution, and who was imprisoned here shortly before his execution in 1898. As well as his cell, the site includes a pleasant, peaceful garden, and views across the Pasig River to Binondo, the crowded, bustling Chinatown that stands on the river's northern shore. Binondo is a good place to come to explore the colourful markets that line the narrow streets and practically fill the square outside Quiapo Church.

Above: A dusk view of some of the tower blocks of Makati, one of the main centres of modern Metro Manila and its commercial heart.

Opposite: The Church of San Agustin, venerable relic of the Spanish colonial era, is the oldest church in the Philippines, and the only Hispanic building in Intramuros to survive fighting at the end of the Second World War.

RIZAL PARK AND ITS MUSEUMS

Anyone who wants to learn a little more about Rizal's execution need do no more than leave Intramuros by its southern, main gate, cross the golf course that rather bizarrely separates Intramuros from the rest of the city, negotiate the maze of main roads that cut through this area, and then find themselves in Rizal Park. A rectangular swathe of very welcome greenery, Rizal Park – more usually known simply as Luneta – has at its western end an enormous memorial, permanently guarded by soldiers, that marks Rizal's execution site. The park's eastern end is marked, in balance with Rizal, by a statue of Lapu-Lapu, the Philippines' first national hero, who killed none other than Ferdinand Magellan, the first man to claim these islands for Spain, back in 1521.

Close by are two enormous neo-classical buildings housing the National Museum of the Filipino People and the National Gallery of Art, both fantastic museums worth exploring. The former houses exhibits both on the Philippines' pre-Hispanic peoples, including what is known about the earliest prehistoric settlers, and on today's numerous cultural groups, particularly in Mindanao. There is also a large exhibit on the *San Diego*, a Spanish galleon that sank in 1600. The Gallery of Art houses both traditional and modern Filipino paintings, the former including the massive *Spoliarium* by Juan Luna, a hero of the anti-Spanish revolution who lived for some time in Italy. The painting depicts a rather violent gladiatorial scene in Rome's Coliseum, a far cry from the far more Philippines-oriented subjects of the gallery's modern paintings.

Luneta itself consists of some very pleasant fountains, tree-shaded areas, an outdoor theatre and a pair of Chinese and Japanese gardens, while to the south stands lovely little Paco Park, a very pretty – and usually peaceful – oasis enclosed within old circular Spanish walls.

Left: Spanish religious relics on show in the National Museum of the Filipino People.

Opposite top: A statue of Lapu-Lapu, first Philippine hero, who killed Magellan. The statue stands in Rizal Park.

Opposite below and left: Two very different displays in the National Museum of the Filipino People, on the left a *kulintaang*, a traditional percussion instrument of the Islamic deep south, and on the right a model of the *San Diego*, a Spanish galleon that sank off the Philippine coast in 1600.

Below: The fountain and chapel in peaceful Paco Park, a small oasis in the heart of Manila.

FOLLOWING THE BAY SHORE

Beyond here it is possible to follow the curving sweep of Manila Bay, heading southwards along a promenade that parallels both the shore and busy Roxas Boulevard. A rather hot excursion during the daytime, this is a great place to walk at sunset, the sun sinking over the sea and the mountains of the Bataan peninsula to the west. The promenade passes the Manila Yacht Club and marina, and then gets a little lost in a promontory that includes the Cultural Center of the Philippines. From here it might be better to grab a taxi and continue southwards to the Mall of Asia, one of Manila's newest developments, a huge shopping mall along a shoreside promenade complete with hundreds of snack stalls, cafes and bars, all lying at the heart of a vast coastal reclamation that is rapidly mushrooming into a whole, brand-new section of the city.

There are few better places in hectic Manila to wind down at the end of your day than on this promenade, watching the dusk sky glow across the water, cooled by a gentle sea breeze, clear (well, almost) of the noise of bellowing traffic.

Above: The concrete facade of the huge Mall of Asia, which faces the sea and a new promenade.

Top: Relaxing at sunset on the promenade along Roxas Boulevard.

Left: Lines of snack stalls and a ferris wheel complete the promenade walk along the seafront outside the Mall of Asia.

Opposite: A dusk view of one of Manila's main arteries, Roxas Boulevard, paralleling the seashore, and separated from it by the promenade.

THE TAAL REGION

AN ACTIVE VOLCANIC LANDSCAPE

Just a couple of hours' drive southwards out of Manila brings you to a wholly different environment, that of Taal volcano and its enormous caldera lake. The approach to this stunning scenery is through pleasantly verdant countryside that gently slopes upwards, but that gives no clue as to the spectacle that will soon be unveiled. For the last couple of kilometres, as the road enters the town of Tagaytay, the climb becomes quite steep, and suddenly it reaches a ridge, beyond which the land drops away dramatically in almost sheer, but nevertheless largely forested slopes, revealing a view of breathtaking proportions, sweeping across a vast lake several hundred metres below. You have arrived at the Taal caldera and one of the Philippines' most famous views, that of Taal Lake seen from Tagaytay.

TAGAYTAY AND THE TAAL CALDERA

The lake fills the floor of the enormous Taal caldera, at about 30 km (19 miles) in diameter, a huge volcanic crater surrounded by rocky walls over 600 m (2,000 ft) high. Tagaytay lies strung out along a large part of the northern section of the caldera rim, an attractive, relaxed town that attracts streams of visitors both for its views and its relatively cool air. At 752 m (2,474 ft) above sea level, Tagaytay is significantly more comfortable than sticky Manila, especially at night.

Arguably, the best view of all is to be found at the suitably named Taal Vista Hotel, at Tagaytay's western end. With a completely clear, unhindered view of the whole lake, from here its full vastness – covering about 270 sq km (104 square miles) – can clearly be seen. The lake is almost wholly enclosed by cliffs and hills, the furthest, southern shore rising up into the peak of 930-m (3,060-ft) Mt Maculot. Only along a small part of the lake's south-west shore do the surrounding cliffs drop away into low-lying ground, an area that was once under sea water, linking today's lake with the open sea.

Directly in line between Mt Maculot and Tagaytay sits an island, relatively low-lying and initially rather innocuous-looking. Innocuous-looking, that is, until you notice the craters that pockmark its surface. This is Volcano Island, site of today's active Taal Volcano, and although it is barely 5 km (three miles) long it is covered with no fewer than 47 cones and craters.

TAAL VOLCANO'S ERUPTIONS

Though one of the world's smallest volcanoes, it is also one of the Philippines' most dangerous. With nearly 40 eruptions recorded since 1572 (when records began), Taal is highly active and has been frequently deadly. Two of its biggest eruptions were in 1784 and 1911,

Right: In January 2020, Taal Volcano finally – after lying quiet for nearly 50 years – launched into a spectacular eruption that blanketed the entire area in smoke and ash. Residents of Volcano Island had to flee for their lives, while tens of thousands of people around the shores of Taal Lake were evacuated for fear of worse to come.

Opposite: A dramatic sunrise view across Taal Lake and over Taal's Volcano Island, seen from the town of Tagaytay. Although shot before the January 2020 eruption, the silhouette outline of Volcano Island has changed little, even though the island's vegetation has been largely lost.

both resulting in major loss of life and destruction of towns.

Taal went through a period of activity in the 1960s and 70s, and then went quiet unil January 2020, when its main crater erupted for over a week, resulting in evacuation of tens of thousands of people living all around the caldera. A major eruption seemed imminent, but to date it hasn't materialised.

At the time of writing (June 2023), although the latest eruption was in March 2022, the volcano remains restless, with regular shallow tremors, and daily clouds of sulphur dioxide released, resulting in widespread acidic volcano fog, or *vog* as it has become known.

Not surprisingly, Volcano Island remains firmly off-limits, but grandstand views are still possible from the surrounding Taal caldera rim, particularly from the area around Tagaytay.

EXPLORING TAAL LAKE NEAR TAGAYTAY AND TALISAY

Despite their proximity to the active Volcano Island, it is perfectly possible to visit and explore Tagaytay and the nearby lakeside village of Talisay.

Both suffered badly during the 2020 eruption, being buried in layers of ash, Talisay's lake-based tourism economy destroyed. Today, the communities are recovering, local vegetation – badly damaged by the acidic ash – is returning, and the tourism economy is picking up.

Grandstand views of the smouldering volcano are everywhere around Tagaytay, though sometimes partially obscured by ash and/or *vog* (those with respiratory conditions should take care). Down at Talisay, boat trips onto the lake now seem to be possible, though they stay well away from Volcano Island.

Right: With the 2020 and 2022 Taal eruptions, the lakeside village of Talisay suffered evacuation, huge amounts of damage, and a collapse of its tourism-based economy (already suffering from the Covid shutdown). Today, both the village and surrounding vegetation are recovering, with lakeside tourism and some boat rides on the lake once again possible.

Below: A view across Volcano Island about a year after the 2020 eruptions shows a dramatic remodelling of the central part of the island (on the left of the image), with the vegetation largely stripped away, though already returning to some parts.

THE SOUTH SIDE OF TAAL LAKE

To the south-west of Taal Lake there is a gap in the surrounding caldera walls, and it is here that the lake has its one and only outlet, the River Pansipit flowing out of the lake and down to the sea at Balayan Bay, less than 10 km (six miles) away. Until the 18th century the lake was an inlet of the sea, but a succession of eruptions sealed it off, leaving the lake we see today. Over the intervening years, its salinity has decreased until it has become freshwater, leading a number of trapped marine fish species to evolve to live there. Several have sadly become extinct, but today there are still the world's only freshwater sardine (known locally as *tawilis*), a freshwater trevally (called *maliputo*) and the venomous Garman sea-snake. All three are under pressure from over-fishing and pollution, but efforts are underway to protect them.

Until 1754, San Nicolas was the site of the town of Taal, but in that year the settlement was destroyed by the volcano's largest-ever eruption, after which the town was rebuilt 10 km (six miles) to the south-west, on the shores of Balayan Bay. A massive church was built in the new town, and although it had to be rebuilt again in the 1850s, today the huge Basilica of St Martin de Tours stands strong, proud and spectacular, said to be one of Asia's largest churches, the centrepiece of today's Taal town. A climb to the top of its belfry is worth the effort

Above right: The facade of the Basilica of St Martin de Tours, a Spanish-era church dating from the 1850s, at the heart of Taal town.

Right: The magnificent nave of the Basilica of St Martin de Tours, in Taal town, said to be one of the largest churches in Asia.

Opposite top: A view from the top of the Basilica's belfry across a residential part of Taal town to the sea in Balayan Bay.

Opposite below: The River Pansipit is Taal Lake's only outlet, flowing sluggishly to the sea just 10km (six miles) away.

for its fantastic views, the upper half of Binitiang Malaki clearly visible above the caldera walls to the north, the sea glistening a short distance to the west, the town inbetween for all the world looking like a scene from the Caribbean.

If that were not enough, Taal has become quite a cultural centre due to the high number of colonial-era houses that have survived, specifically protected as both heritage icons and one-time homes for some of the heroes of the anti-Spanish revolution. The town is also well known for its hand-crafted embroidery using silk, cotton and native cloths such as those derived from pineapple fibres. The best place to see this is the central market, where a plethora of shops and stalls show off some spectacular clothes.

Both San Nicolas and Taal town suffered badly during the January 2020 eruption, both having to be evacuated, and a dense, thick and highly corrosive layer of ash landing on the settlements and causing extensive damage. Today, life is returning to normal, though the volcano and its continued emissions remain a constant threat.

SOUTHERN BICOL

WHALE SHARKS TO VOLCANOES

Bicol, the southern part of Luzon, is a lively part of the Pacific Ring of Fire, site of a string of active volcanoes. The southernmost region has two of the liveliest, the forest-draped Mt Bulusan and a little further north the mighty Mt Mayon towering ominously over the city of Legazpi. Between the two sits the coastal town of Donsol, arguably the country's main centre for watching and interacting with the world's largest fish, the huge Whale Shark. This is really a part of the Philippines for getting up close and dirty with two of the most magnificent opposite extremes of nature.

GETTING CLOSE TO MT MAYON

At 2,462 m (8,692 ft), Mayon is one of the Philippines' highest mountains, famous for its absolutely perfect, iconic volcano shape, sweeping from sea level straight up to its pointed summit in a spectacular arc.

Unfortunately, Mayon is also the Philippines' most active volcano, with over 50 eruptions in the past 500 years, the most recent in 2018. Fortunately, because it erupts so frequently those eruptions are in general relatively small, at least by the standards of most active volcanoes, which is why it maintains its near-perfect volcano shape. At the time of writing (June 2023), Mayon seems to be building up towards another eruption, which could happen at any time.

Mayon's instability does mean that it is the most closely monitored of all the country's 22 active volcanoes, which in turn means that you cannot actually get all that close to it. The Philippine Institute of Volcanology and Seismology (PHIVOLCS), the body charged with monitoring the Philippines' volcanoes, maintains a six-kilometre (four-mile) radius Permanent Danger Zone around the summit that no-one is supposed to enter.

Although some hiking on Mayon's lower slopes is possible, a popular alternative is to take a quad-bike ride from Cagsawa, at Mayon's south-western foot, up to the lower edge of Mayon's lowest petrified lava flow. Coming to a halt just short of the tree line, and barely a few kilometres from the first of the villages, to this day much of the lava is still black and devoid of vegetation, its lowest limit marked by a sheer wall of black rock.

Right: The huge, conical and smouldering summit of Mt Mayon, the Philippines' most active volcano, towers ominously above the suburbs of Legazpi, one of the largest cities in Bicol, in the far south of Luzon.

IN MAYON'S SHADOW

Having Mt Mayon as a neighbour makes for uncomfortable living. Cagsawa was once a prosperous village, until an eruption in 1814 destroyed the settlement. Today, the ruins remain as a picturesque testament to Mayon's power. The main feature is the church's bell tower, all that remains recognizable of the church, together with a number of the village's walls. Beyond the stone ruins rice fields stretch into the distance, with Mayon as a gently smouldering backdrop.

The modern port city of Legazpi, to the south of Mayon and sitting on Bicol's Pacific coast, manages to fair better, though with the volcano's towering cone dominating the city's skyline, the ominous threat is always visible. For the visitor, however, it makes for one of the most spectacular skylines imaginable. There are some terrific viewpoints from which to take in the volcanic urban landscape, such as Sleeping Lion Hill just south of the port, the eastern breakwater of the port itself, Lignon Hill north of the city and the terrace outside the magnificent church in Daraga, a suburb to the north-west of Legazpi.

Being right on the coast and rising from sea level straight up into a huge mountain, Mayon inevitably attracts a vast amount of cloud, and so spends much of its time at least partially cloaked. To heighten the chances of seeing Mayon in all her clear, threatening beauty, largely free of cloud, it is best to visit during the March–May relatively dry period.

Above right: The facade of the historic Spanish-era church in Daraga, a suburb of Legazpi. The terrace fronting the church has superb views of Mt Mayon.

Right: A ruined church tower is one of the few remnants of the village of Cagsawa, sitting at the south-west foot of Mt Mayon, and destroyed by an eruption in 1814.

Opposite top: The downtown area of Legazpi, sitting on Bicol's Pacific east coast, is the economic heart of the region.

Opposite below: The active summit of Mt Bulusan creates a picturesque view across the calm waters of Bulusan Lake, on the southern slopes of the volcano.

MT BULUSAN: MAYON'S SMALLER COUSIN

Sitting on Bicol's final southernmost peninsula is Mt Bulusan, another highly active volcano. At 1,559 m (5,129 ft), it is significantly smaller than Mayon, but it seems to be almost as active, constantly under the watchful gaze of PHIVOLCS. Like Mayon, there is an almost permanent ban on hiking anywhere near the summit slopes, but unlike Mayon, population pressures are rather less severe. The lowlands surrounding Bulusan are intensively farmed and the small town of Irosin sits just at the volcano's southern foot, but its steep slopes are mostly wrapped in rainforest, that are protected as an important national park.

Although much of the volcano is off-limits, one area that is open and really worth exploring is Bulusan Lake. A lovely caldera lake sitting a few hundred metres up Mt Bulusan's southern slopes, it is surrounded by dense, vibrant rainforest. A footpath follows the lake shore all the way round, giving a rare opportunity to explore some unusually accessible forest. Early in the morning and late in the afternoon are the best times to explore, to see lizards scurrying away across the path, and to look out for some relatively rare Philippine forest birds, including hornbills and the Philippine Frogmouth. Along the lake shore, there are regular views of Bulusan's summit cone standing above the forested slopes, to the north of the lake. Unfortunately, the smouldering, active crater is not visible from here – for that the best views are from the Sorsogon-Irosin main road, on Bulusan's west flank.

THE WHALE SHARKS OF DONSOL

When the presence of large concentrations of Whale Sharks in the sheltered waters off the fishing town of Donsol, on Bicol's west coast, was first reported to the wider world in the late 1990s, no-one could quite believe it. It was not long, however, before the local fishermen started to organize boat trips out to see the Whale Sharks, and today they are one of Bicol's star attractions.

Whale Sharks gather here for a few months every year, generally from November to March, presumably to feed on the vast amounts of plankton that, unfortunately, make the water rather cloudy. The shark-watching trips are well organized, a daily limited number of boats heading out, mostly early in the morning, for about 90 minutes, with each boat crewed by a team of experienced spotters and a biologist.

Snorkelling with the Whale Sharks is a fantastic experience, the biologist ensuring that everyone gets off the boat and into position in the water each time a Whale Shark is spotted approaching. It is possible to swim alongside them for some distance, though sometimes they are easily disturbed: once they have had enough of your presence they usually dive into the murky depths and out of sight.

The cloudiness of Donsol's water does create some visibility problems. While a Whale Shark swimming near the surface may be perfectly visible from a boat, once you are in the water it can become almost impossible to track its movement. One moment you are looking at empty water, the next you have a huge 15-m (49-ft) long animal with a gaping plankton-sieving mouth coming straight at you. When this behemoth glides past barely a couple of metres away – usually cruising along at a speed that you can just keep pace with – the poor visibility can make it difficult to see both head and tail simultaneously.

The crystal-clear, Whale Shark-tracking waters of such places as Australia this certainly is not, but nevertheless the joy and excitement of being in the water with Donsol's Whale Sharks are high octane stuff. During the high season, it is indeed one of the easiest places in the world to go Whale Shark-watching. Although sightings are never guaranteed, of course, on a good day it is possible to jump in the water and swim with five of six of these giants in the space of a couple of hours: an experience not to be missed!

Above: Waiting to be picked up after spending a few exhilarating minutes snorkelling with a Whale Shark.

Left: A Whale Shark-adorned jeepney in Donsol, a town where tours to watch these marine creatures are big business.

Far left: A huge Whale Shark cruises along just beneath the sea's surface a kilometre or two off the Donsol coast.

SIARGAO ISLAND

SURFING ON CLOUD NINE

Welcome to surfing heaven, Philippines style. This triangular island lying off the north-east coast of Mindanao is the country's lead surfing spot, the Pacific swell sending in some fabulous rollers along the fringing coral reefs of this exposed, east-facing coastline. In the 20-plus years since Australian surfers in search of the next great surf break stumbled upon Siargao, the island has gone from total obscurity to life as *the* premier surfing venue, not just in the Philippines, but in the whole of Southeast Asia, firmly entrenched in the international surfing competition circuit and drawing more and more people from ever further afield.

LIFE ON CLOUD NINE

So amazed were those early pioneers by the quality of the surf breaks close to Siargao's south-eastern tip that they named it Cloud Nine, and it seems that the surfers have been living the dream ever since. The epithet stuck, to the point that even the local Filipinos took it up, and pretty soon no-one could remember what the area had been originally called. Now it is only Cloud Nine, a name synonymous with surfing.

Originally, it was just the surf break, waves rolling in across a reef a few hundred metres offshore, but soon the name Cloud Nine was applied to the landward side of those waves, initially little more than a typical Philippine shoreline: a few strips of sand alternating with coralline rocks and mangroves, backed by coconut palms and beach forest. Gradually, as some of the surfers started to put down roots, so a few small resorts started to spring up among the palms, and then a road linking them to the nearest town, General Luna, a few kilometres to the south.

More than 25 years later, and Cloud Nine has turned into quite a resort village, though still laid-back, with a string of lodges, resorts, shops and restaurants lining the road. The cool, surfer-dude culture is still very much alive and well here – not just among both visiting and resident foreigners, but also among the swelling band of home-grown surfers and is likely to continue to dominate the atmosphere for many years to come. Nevertheless, today more and more non-surfers are heading for Cloud Nine, some to try out this great watersport, others simply to find a nice beach or a great escape.

Left: A boardwalk enables surfers at Cloud Nine to walk out to the waves, avoiding a long and tiring paddle, while the three-storey platform at the end provides a terrific viewpoint for spectators.

Opposite: A dusk view of the attractive thatched bungalows of Alon Resort, one of Cloud Nine's most well-established places to stay, situated right by the beach and the start of the surfers' boardwalk.

Development has made life a lot easier for the surfers, not just in terms of some great accommodation and eating choices, but even in reaching those waves. In the early days, surfers had a long and tiring paddle from the beach, across a lagoon, over the reef and finally into the waves. Today, a long, if rickety, boardwalk cuts out all that paddling, enabling surfers, both masters and novices, to jump straight in among the waves. A three-storey pavilion at the end of the boardwalk also provides fantastic ringside seats for the spectators. And for those who just cannot face manhandling their surfboard on and off planes and/or ferries, today Cloud Nine has plenty for hire. And that, of course, also makes it possible for the local surfers to run ever more popular surfing lessons for the uninitiated visitors.

Surfing is possible almost the whole year, but the months from July to October generally have the best waves, a time of year when typhoons passing further north (Siargao is below the typhoon belt) send in enormous Pacific swells. The worst time is probably from November or December through to March, when the north-east monsoon is blowing, sending rain across north-east Mindanao. Cloud Nine hosts a couple of international surfing contests in September, ensuring that the place becomes quite crowded, sending accommodation prices soaring upwards.

LIFE BEYOND THE SURFING

For quite some time the surfers have been using the local *bancas* to get out to the many surf spots that exist up and down Siargao's east coast, well beyond Cloud Nine. The non-surfers too, have started to use them, searching out and exploring some of the many small islands that lie to the south of Siargao. Although Cloud Nine does have some lovely sandy beaches, they are rather small and fragmented, so visitors often head out at least as far as Guyam, a small islet to the south – actually little more than a sandbar with a bunch of coconut palms on it – that is completely ringed by a beautiful white beach. A little further on is the island of Daco, site of a fishing village and a wonderful beach.

Some of the islands, especially Guyam, have shallow reefs that are good for snorkelling, with interesting hard and soft corals and a collection of reef fish. Siargao has not, traditionally, been a place for scuba diving, but that is changing, with a couple of dive centres now operating, and a growing number of good dive sites slowly being discovered. What Siargao does have, which is unusual in the Philippines, is deep-sea angling, with a number of boats available for hire, taking anglers out on day trips into some of the nearby deeper Pacific waters. To the south-west lies Bucas Grande Island, site of picturesque Sohoton Cave and lagoon, an increasingly visited place and readily reached by *banca*.

Above: A local surfer shows how it is supposed to be done, even on a relatively calm day at Cloud Nine.

Left: Newcomers get an introductory lesson in the art of balancing a surfboard, in the shallows at Cloud Nine.

Opposite: The lovely, enticing shoreline at Cloud Nine, seen from the start of the surfers' boardwalk.

EXPLORING THE ISLAND

Most of Siargao's action is focussed in and around Cloud Nine, with much of the rest of the island seeing only limited benefit. Everyone staying at Cloud Nine will get to sample the joys of General Luna, universally abbreviated to simply GL. It is a ramshackle little place, consisting of a small grid of dusty streets, dilapidated buildings, a huge church, a long beach covered with a host of *bancas*, and a very long jetty, but after even just a few days in Cloud Nine, GL can feel like the great metropolis.

Siargao's main town and port is Dapa, lying on the island's south coast. Anyone arriving by ferry from the mainland town of Surigao will pass through Dapa, probably immediately being scooped up by a driver and whisked off to Cloud Nine and so seeing very little of the town. But because of the island's road network, for anyone wanting to explore Siargao, Dapa is an important starting or waypoint, anyone hiring a vehicle from Cloud Nine and GL probably having to come through Dapa.

From here up the west coast, the road leads to the town of Del Carmen, jumping-off point for some really interesting boat tours around a huge mangrove forest, with its maze of waterways and emerald green trees, and at 8,600 ha (21,240 acres) Mindanao's largest. This is one of the few remaining wild homes in the Philippines for the huge Philippine Crocodile, though the chances of seeing one are tiny.

At Siargao's north-eastern tip are the villages of Sta Monica and Burgos, and running between these two is a truly spectacular white sandy beach, with surf crashing onto a fringing reef a few hundred metres offshore. It is a truly stunning sight, and yet it is practically deserted, the preserve almost wholly of fishermen and little children. A couple of very small resorts have been built near the villages, though they seem lost in the vastness of the beach, and it is clear that few people venture this far, at least to stay overnight. But could this beach be the next big Siargao destination?

Above right: The calm, sheltered mangroves at Del Carmen, on Siargao's west coast, are a protected area, the largest mangrove forest in Mindanao and one of the few remaining homes in the Philippines for the Philippine Crocodile.

Right: Coconut palms and moored *bancas* along the shore at the east coast town of General Luna, seen during an unusually high tide, when even the palms became inundated.

Opposite: The spectacular and almost deserted beach at Santa Monica on Siargao's north-east coast has barely a single lodge or resort along it despite its great beauty.

DAVAO

CAPITAL OF THE DEEP SOUTH

Nestling in the sheltered waters of the huge and highly indented Davao Gulf, the city of Davao is by far Mindanao's largest, the third most important conurbation in the Philippines after Metro Manila and Cebu City. Although this is a largely Christian city, the Spanish did not take over this area until the second half of the 19th century, ensuring that their historic stamp is much weaker here than in much of the country. Instead of finding Spanish-era churches and villas scattered among the 20th century concrete buildings, in Davao you will find only modern churches plus the occasional mosque and a few Malay-style houses. Davao, although it is very much anchored in the Filipino Christian culture of the Philippines, is in a transition zone into the more Islamic areas of the country's southern edge.

Davao City extends over such a vast land area that officially it is the Philippines' largest city, though much of it covers farmland, plantations and mountains, as well as the city itself. The urban area nestles in the south-east corner, along the coast, leaving the northern and western parts covered with forested mountains, including – in the far west – Mt Apo Natural Park, at 2,956 m (9,725 ft) the Philippines' highest mountain, clearly visible from the city, though too far away to be said to actually tower over it.

For the visitor, although the urban area contains plenty of good hotels, these serve largely as a base for exploring the area. The city itself has only a few things of any interest; most of Davao's attractions lying around the fringes, along the coast and in the countryside.

Above right: An ornamental gateway marks the entrance to Davao's crowded Chinatown, opposite the popular Magsaysay Park.

Right: Philippine Crocodiles, largely submerged and almost hidden by algae, in a pond at the Davao Crocodile Park.

Opposite: A lively display of some of the traditions of Mindanao's Islamic cultural groups, in the Museo Dabawenyo, a small museum in the city centre.

EXPLORING DAVAO

The urban area consists of a grid of streets laid out to the north of the mouth of the Davao River, with the main centre around the modernist concrete behemoth that is San Pedro Cathedral. Close by are the small, but attractive and refreshingly green space of Osmeña Park and the dusty but interesting Museo Dabawenyo, a museum to the life and history of Davao and its peoples, including many of the Muslim groups that live in southern Mindanao.

Away to the east is the cramped and crowded commercial district of Davao's Chinatown, and beyond that, along the city's eastern shore is Magsaysay Park, a moderately large expanse of trees, cafes and shoreside promenade that an awful lot of people head for to chill out. To the south, stretching along the shore for quite some distance, is a fishing village, a rather ramshackle place of self-built houses, many on stilts above the water, with a few small mosques here and there. Similar housing can be seen along the shores of the Davao River.

Just south of Magsaysay Park's entrance is a small market, which, along with the main Bankerohan Public Market in the west of the city, is a good place to check out one of Davao's most famous products, durian. Arguably the city's biggest agricultural product, Davao is often said to be the durian capital of the Philippines, a reputation that is something of a double-edge sword. A big, hard-cased and very spiky fruit, durian is, one has to say, an acquired taste. While its flesh has a rich, sweet and almost creamy taste, the fruit as a whole has a rather heady, sewer-like aroma. It is no coincidence that throughout Southeast Asia, airlines ban durian from their planes. Anyone trying durian for the first time could try holding their nose to get past the smell and so taste the fruit!

A short distance off Davao's eastern shore sits Samal Island, the city's beachside play area, rather quiet during the week, but crowded at weekends. With a string of beaches, the island's shores are lined with coconut palms and resorts, though those along the west coast have a less than exotic view across to Davao's port and chemical-plant facilities. Resorts out on the east coast have a much better tropical, away-from-it-all feel to them, even though they are not really all that far away from the city.

On the city's northern fringes you come to the Davao Crocodile Park, a zoo-cum-captive breeding centre for the highly endangered Philippine Crocodile. Far more of these huge reptiles live here than anyone could possibly ever meet in the wild, all easily viewed from the safety of a network of raised walkways. Other animals kept here include ostriches and the Philippine Brown Deer, while nearby is an attractive butterfly park, a garden of dense vegetation enclosed within netting.

THE PHILIPPINE EAGLE CENTER

Heading north or west from the urban area quickly leads into the heart of the Mindanao countryside, a verdant landscape of banana, coconut, durian, pineapple and citrus fruit groves, along with some of the Philippines' only rubber plantations.

Almost 40 km (25 miles) north of the city, near the village of Malagos, at a point where the farmlands and villages finally start to give way to mountains and rainforest, sits the Philippine Eagle Center, a captive-breeding site for this highly endangered raptor. The world's second largest eagle and unique to the Philippines, only a few hundred remain in the wild, very thinly spread across the country's most remote forests, their numbers brought down by hunting and loss of habitat. Since the early 1990s the Philippine Eagle Foundation has struggled to conserve the species through a combination of field work and research into captive breeding, the latter carried out at this Malagos site. Over the past few years, they have started to have success with the breeding, to the point now that almost 40 eagles have been born here. Initial steps towards the long-term goal of releasing captively bred eagles back into the wild have been partially successful, but there is still a long way to go with this programme.

For the visitor, the Center is a wonderful place to explore, a beautiful garden and forest setting in which a number of Philippine eagles can be seen, both inside cages and out. Other animals housed here, and which can be easily seen, include Brahminy Kites, White-bellied Sea-eagles, Philippine Warty Pigs and Philippine Brown Deer, along with several other raptors, some of which are unique to the Philippines.

Right: A Philippine Eagle, sometimes also called the Monkey-eating Eagle, over a metre tall, sits on a perch in the Philippine Eagle Center at Malagos.

Above right: The Philippine Eagle Center also houses a number of Brahminy Kites, much smaller than the eagle, and also much more common in the wild, widespread across South and Southeast Asia.

Opposite: Far more than just a collection of Philippine birds of prey, the Philippine Eagle Center is also a lovely tropical garden, worth exploring simply for its own sake.

THE GREENS OF EDEN

Away to the west of Malagos, on the slopes of Mt Talomo, a north-eastern outrider of Mt Apo, lies Eden, a very popular parkland that was created just a few years ago from an eroding, denuded mountain slope reforested with pines. While it would be nice to have the native forest back, the new covering of pines is hugely successful and a very pleasant environment, and at an altitude of several hundred metres is much less hot and humid than coastal Davao. A mix of restaurants, ziplines, fishing lake, parkland and pine woodland walks, complete with accommodation, this is a very relaxing and refreshing place to come. For a taste of the native rainforest that once covered this entire site, there is still a sliver that escaped the chainsaw, hunkering down in a narrow river valley, through which there are a number of good walks. Although this rainforest fragment consists mostly of native forest plants, a few introduced heliconia plants have crept in, their presence given away by their remarkable red and yellow flowers.

This is a lovely spot, and although it is not perfect, it is a wonderful antidote to the steaming urban congestion down on the coast.

Right: The red flower of a Heliconia plant at Eden. Although Eden's remaining rainforest contains many Heliconias, they must have been introduced as they are not normal in Philippine forests, but instead are typical of Central and South America and the Caribbean.

Opposite: The angling lake is a popular attraction at Eden.

Below: A suspension bridge spans the river that flows through Eden's surviving rainforest, a great place for some hiking.

MINDORO AND PALAWAN

THE WILD FRONTIER

Covering the Philippines' western fringes, the Mindoro and Palawan island groupings take in some of the wildest and most remote parts of the country. This is the land of adventure and eco-tourism, and the places visited in this part of our journey through the country reflect that.

The most accessible part of Mindoro is Puerto Galera, also one of the country's longest established tourism destinations; a place of beaches, forested mountains and some of the healthiest coral reefs (and hence best diving) in the country.

On crossing over to Palawan, we start in the northernmost region, the remote Calamian Islands, and in particular the islands of Busuanga, Coron, Calauit and Dimakya, a region renowned for its coralline, limestone rock formations and lagoons, wreck diving and an African wildlife park.

From here we join the Palawan mainland, stopping initially in the far north at El Nido, site of the stunning Bacuit Bay, with its beaches and rocky coral islands, perfect for playing Robinson Crusoe on. Further south lies the Puerto Princesa Subterranean River, a mountainous national park that is the site of a famous underground river, as well as forests, mangroves and easily spotted wildlife. Our final destination in this section is Honda Bay, another site of coral islands, this time absolutely flat, ringed by sand and mangroves; the quintessential desert islands.

Left: A dusk view of the hills that enclose the much-indented Coron Bay, across to Culion Island, and seen from Mt Tapyas, high above Coron Town, on Busuanga Island.

PUERTO GALERA

THE PORT OF GALLEONS

A ferry ride from Luzon's Batangas port across the Verde Island Passage to northern Mindoro brings us to beautiful Puerto Galera, one of the Philippines' leading resort areas. Here, a verdant, rather hammerhead-shaped peninsula grouped with a cluster of islands forms a perfect natural harbour, the deep blue waters almost completely enclosed by coconut palm-clad hills. When the Spanish discovered it in the 17th century it quickly became a favoured anchorage and a place for repairing their galleons. The name Puerto Galera – Port of Galleons – was born.

Today, it remains a favoured anchorage, though this time for a cluster of beautiful yachts, lying on moorings a short distance off the waterfront of the peninsula's main town, Muelle. Most ferries come and go from here, a steady stream generally of powerful *bancas* running locals and visitors alike between Puerto Galera and Batangas. Muelle's setting is stunning. Arriving by ferry, the hidden natural harbour slowly reveals itself as you pass through narrow channels separating the peninsula to the east from the islands to the west. Finally, Muelle's harbourfront gradually comes into view at its innermost end. First seen are a sea wall and jetty, with most of the *banca* ferries pulling up to the former. Behind is a line of stalls selling snacks and handicrafts, alongside which the jeepneys and tricycles pull up.

MOUNTAINS, BEACHES AND CORALS

Puerto Galera is renowned for two things – its beaches and the quality of its submarine environment, a string of magnificent coral reefs attracting divers from around the world. Inland, the coastline is backed by forest-clad mountains that rise up to the summits of Mts Talipanan and Malasimbo, the latter being the highest at 1,228 m (4,029 ft). UNESCO declared the entire area to be a Man and the Biosphere Reserve as far back as 1977, but despite this protection deforestation on the mountains has been extensive (though some good areas remain), and uncontrolled tourism developments have resulted in significant damage to the coastal areas, including some of the coral reefs. Nevertheless, growing efforts to protect the reefs have ensured that many are still in very good condition and worthy of their high reputation.

Despite the beauty of its setting, Muelle tends to be a transit point for visitors, who are then ferried out to Puerto Galera's resorts: either those on the peninsula, or those along the main coast, mostly to the west of Muelle. Divers generally head for the resorts on the peninsula as these are much closer to the best reefs, while those in search of the best beaches go to those along the coast. Unfortunately, the best diving resorts have the worst beaches, while the best beaches are a long way from the best dive sites, so visitors have to choose their main priority!

Right: Yachts on moorings in the calm, sheltered waters of Puerto Galera's natural harbour at Muelle.

Opposite: The coconut palm-lined beach at Small La Laguna, bathed in evening sunlight, may not be the Philippines' most beautiful stretch of sand, but it does have some of the best diving facilities.

PUERTO GALERA'S DIVING AREAS

Most of the dive resorts are clustered in three small bays at the far end of the peninsula. Called Big La Laguna, Small La Laguna and Sabang Beaches, none of these has a beach to get excited about, but they do have some of the Philippines' best diving facilities, as well as plenty of after-diving entertainment. The resorts and bars at Sabang in particular are well known for their partying, so those who prefer the quiet life generally head either for the two La Laguna beaches or one of the more exclusive resorts hidden away among the peninsula's secluded coves.

Although this area is principally dedicated to diving, there are also a few good snorkelling sites. The leader among these is the Coral Gardens, a shallow area just a few metres deep, that lies off the western tip of Medio Island.

The main dive sites lie along and close to the peninsula's coast, mostly little more than a few minutes by boat from the resorts. The sites at the peninsula's western end are generally in calm, sheltered conditions, particularly those around Medio and Boquete Islands, while those to the east, especially around Escarceo Point – the peninsula's north-eastern tip – can become quite rough and subject to strong currents. On all of them, both gentle and steep drop-offs are covered with a wide diversity of hard and soft corals, anemones and sponges, as well as a vast wealth of technicolour reef fish, ranging from the delicate yellow-and-black Moorish Idols and orange-and-white striped clownfish, to the downright oddly shaped batfish and sweetlips, as well as a host of different types of triggerfish.

Above: Sea fans are a common sight on the steep submarine slopes, usually at a depth of about 20 metres, typically found off the northeastern coast of Puerto Galera.

THE WESTERN BEACHES

To the west of Muelle are three beautiful beaches, which are, from east to west, White Beach, Aninuan and Talipanan. The first of these is a huge, spectacular stretch of white sand, and this is where most of the area's accommodation is. Unfortunately, the development has been poorly managed, with the result that resorts are now crammed in together, with little space and no sense of design. In short, it is rather ugly. So, it is fortunate that the beach is so huge and can easily accommodate the numbers of people that come to stay here, particularly at the weekends.

A couple of kilometres to the west lies Aninuan town, and another long and stunning stretch of white sand. A small handful of resorts cluster together at the far eastern end of the beach, but the vast majority of the land behind the sands remains untouched. The reason for this lack of development is that much of it has been bought by the Ayala family, one of the wealthiest in the Philippines, and on part of it they have built a large and rather attractive house for their own use. Whether they will eventually develop the remainder as a resort or leave it in its present virgin state remains to be seen, but for the moment at least the result is that Aninuan beach is mostly deserted and extremely beautiful.

Walking around a small headland at the western end of Aninuan beach brings you to Talipanan, the last of the three beaches. Development here has also been quite light, though the crumbling ruins of a number of failed beachfront resorts rather spoil the view of an otherwise near-perfect beach. The few resorts that Talipanan does have lie mostly at its western end, close to the village of the same name. This place is quite the antithesis to crowded, noisy White Beach: at Talipanan life is laid back and very slow. Few people make it this far along the coast.

Above: A bar-cum-diving centre is a great place to unwind in the evening, along the sands of White Beach.

Left: The huge expanse of White Beach in evening sunlight, backed by the vast bulk of Mt Talipanan.

There are some possibilities for heading inland from these three beaches to explore the forested mountains that tower over the resorts. For those feeling adventurous, it is possible to go hiking on Mt Malasimbo, though it is essential to take a local guide. Far simpler is the 30-minute trek from Talipanan up to Talipanan Falls. It is not the world's largest waterfall, but it is beautiful in its diminutive way, and the trek up gives a good opportunity to experience some of the rainforest. The path is quite easy to follow – a guide is not needed – and in its early stages passes through a village of Mangyan people, the native inhabitants of Mindoro. The Mangyan have traditionally kept themselves fairly separate from Philippine society, but those at Talipanan have become rather more integrated, with the arrival of schools and skills training, resulting in them using their traditional basket-weaving skills to produce craftwork for the visitor market.

From Puerto Galera, few people venture further into Mindoro, the island having a reputation for being rather wild and remote, its roads less than enjoyable to travel along. Although there are a number of places along the west coast really worth visiting, these are generally reached directly from Manila by air. Few people travel overland from Puerto Galera.

Above: Mangyan women work on traditional baskets in their village at Talipanan.

Top: The beach at Talipanan is quiet and laid-back, the most remote of Puerto Galera's beaches and host to just a handful of resorts.

Opposite: Lovely, diminutive Talipanan falls lies in rainforest about 30 minutes on foot from Talipanan village.

THE CALAMIAN ISLANDS

PALAWAN'S NORTHERN ISLANDS

Lying off Palawan's northernmost tip, the islands that make up the Calamian group look and feel like one of the Philippines' most remote corners and quietest backwaters. Reached most easily by air from Manila, car ferry from Puerto Princesa (Palawan's capital) or – during the calm summer months – by *banca* ferry from El Nido, this cluster of islands is definitely a place apart, a long way from the hustle of any typical Philippine city.

Though composed of many hundreds of small islands, the great bulk of the Calamian group is made up of one large island, Busuanga, with two more, Coron and Culion, to the south. Created from raised coral reefs, the islands consist almost wholly of coralline limestone rock, giving them a hilly, rocky terrain covered with a thin, poor soil. It is a landscape that becomes quite parched during dry periods when much of the vegetation turns brown and the trees of the few native forests lose their leaves to conserve water.

Beaches are relatively few and far between, much of the coast consisting of coralline cliffs that plunge almost vertically into the sea, and dense mangroves covering most of those shores that are low-lying. A few small beaches do exist, however, notably along the south-west coast of Coron Island, and on a good many of the smaller islands to the north of Busuanga. Inland, Busuanga's landscape is almost wholly rural, scrubby forest alternating with farmland, including a vast area of grazing, Asia's largest cattle ranch.

Coron's landscape, on the other hand, seems to be almost entirely vertical and largely impenetrable, consisting mostly of a jumble of sheer, jagged rock faces and pinnacles, patches of forest clinging on here and there, flat ground quite limited.

Surrounded by rugged hills, Coron Bay is renowned for its wreck diving, the result of a US attack near the end of the Second World War, which sank a convoy of Japanese ships.

Opposite: The aquamarine waters and jagged coralline rocks of Green Lagoon, a sheltered cove on the west coast of Coron Island.

Below: The white sands of Smith Beach, backed by sheer coralline limestone cliffs, are typical of the beaches that lie scattered along Coron Island's south-west coast.

EXPLORING BUSUANGA AND CORON

Busuanga Island is, not surprisingly, the principal entry point for visitors coming to the Calamian Islands, but it is Coron Island that is traditionally the main draw. Busuanga itself has few real attractions, but its main settlement, Coron Town – sitting on Busuanga's south-east coast, not on Coron Island at all – has all the infrastructure and is a pleasant place in itself. It also has a really magnificent viewpoint from the summit of Mt Tapyas, which gives spectacular views not just across Coron Town but also right over Coron Bay to Coron Island to the south-east and Culion Island to the south-west.

Coron Town is the main start and finish point for exploration of the Calamian area. When visitors first started coming here in the 1990s, the main draw was for divers heading to the large number of wrecks submerged in Coron Bay's most enclosed waters, between Busuanga and Culion Islands. All that remains of a convoy of Japanese supply ships sunk by American bombers towards the end of the Second World War, these wrecks continue to be a popular attraction, though with most of them lying in quite deep and cloudy waters, they are generally not for the faint-hearted or the inexperienced.

Along with the wrecks, the most popular destination is Coron Island itself. The entire island is a protected area, declared in the late 1990s to conserve its forested segments and the highly endangered wildlife that lives there. Integral to the protection is a guarantee to safeguard the way of the life of the Tagbanua, an ethnic minority people who call Coron Island home. A rather shy group of people who have always tried to protect their environment, Coron's Tagbanua generally keep themselves to themselves, living in two villages on the island's secluded east coast. It is largely for this reason that much of the island is off-limits, those areas that are open spread along the west coast under licence from the Tagbanua.

Paramount among Coron Island's attractions are Kayangan and Barracuda Lakes, both stunnng pieces of water surrounded by sheer rock walls but accessible by short hikes from the shore. Kayangan in particular gets quite busy these days, but both the lake and the cove that is the access point from the sea continue to be stunningly beautiful. Other sites that can be visited include Green Lagoon, actually a coastal bay with azure waters surrounded by rocky pinnacles covered with emerald green foliage, as well as a number of small beaches, such as Banol, Smith and 91, all along Coron's south-west coast.

Although it is not possible to visit the island's main wildlife areas, in the open parts it is still worth keeping a look out for tortoises crawling around on the forest floor, as well as Palawan Hornbills and Red-vented Cockatoos high up in the trees, the latter now very rare across the Philippines but still reasonably common on Coron Island.

Right: The deep, clear waters of Kayangan Lake have become a very popular place to swim, probably the main visitor attraction on Coron Island.

Opposite: The stunningly lovely cove that is the only access point from the sea to Kayangan Lake, on Coron Island's west coast, has become an icon of the Philippines' natural beauty.

Below: A *banca* carries visitors on a tour along the west coast of Coron Island, in the shadow of coralline limestone cliffs.

HEADING WEST TO CALAUIT

Lying just off the western tip of Busuanga and only separated from it by a mangrove forest and a small bay, Calauit Island is arguably the Philippines' most unusual national park. The explanation is that when the park was initially set up in the late 1970s, it was intended primarily for east African mammals, supposedly a safe haven for what appeared to be increasingly threatened wildlife. To this day, it remains the place to go in the Philippines (if not the whole of Southeast Asia) to see African animals in an entirely natural environment, though admittedly surrounded by the wrong species of vegetation.

Unfortunately, over the years some of the species that were initially introduced have died out, and today all that remain are the giraffes, zebras and eland. The first two are very easy to see as they tend to hang around the main visitor's area, but the eland are almost impossible to find due to their intense shyness. A speciality of Calauit is the option for visitors to hand-feed the giraffes: waving leaf-laden branches is enough to draw their attention, though this is always done in a fenced area – the visitors are fenced in, not the giraffes – to give protection against the possibility of a potentially lethal giraffe kick.

A positive effect of the protection given to the African animals is that the local wildlife has benefitted hugely too. The Calamian Deer, restricted to these islands and almost completely wiped out a few years ago, has undergone a huge recovery on Calauit, to the extent that some

Left: The beachfront bungalows at Club Paradise on Dimakya Island are the perfect place to just relax and enjoy the combination of shade and sea breeze.

Opposite top: A placid early morning view of Calauit Island's southern shore.

Opposite below: A group of zebras wandering at will on the savannah-like grassland of Calauit Island National Park is an unlikely sight.

Below: A vibrantly red and stunningly beautiful *Dendronephthya* species soft tree coral hangs downwards off a submarine cliff close to the shores of Dimakya Island.

deer have been moved to other islands. The deer are a normal part of the landscape here, wandering among the giraffes and zebras, and more or less unafraid of humans. Other Philippine wildlife includes Long-tailed Macaques and mouse deer, the former regularly seen around the island, the latter usually hidden among the undergrowth.

THE NORTHERN ISLANDS

Those in need of some real beach life, along with good coral-reef diving and snorkelling should head to the small islands off Busuanga's north coast, and in particular Dimakya Island, home to Club Paradise, one of the very few accommodation options in this part of the Calamian group. A rather small island, topped by a rocky peak with stunning views, Dimakya has a magnificent beach running along its west shore, which, not surprisingly is where Club Paradise is concentrated.

Quite apart from being a very comfortable resort that is literally well away from everything, this is also a great place for wildlife lovers. Not only do enormous Monitor Lizards wander among the resort's bungalows, but also the trees around the resort are festooned with huge numbers of very noisy, squabbling fruit bats.

A coral reef in quite good condition lies just off the beach, offering good snorkelling, while further afield other islands and reefs provide some fantastic diving opportunities, including the chance to see turtles, rays and the very rare Dugong.

Definitely, this is on my list of favourites.

EL NIDO

A MINIATURE ARCHIPELAGO

A beautiful calm bay, evening sunlight shimmering golden across the waters, a scattering of rocky islands silhouetted against the low light, the sea gently lapping onto the sandy beach... This is what comes into my mind when I think of the words 'El Nido'. It is undoubtedly one of the most beautiful places in the Philippines, backing Bacuit Bay, a quiet part of the world, close to the northern tip of Palawan's main island.

The whole of Bacuit Bay is ringed by high, mostly forested, coralline limestone hills, and across the bay is a vast number of islands, ranging from tiny rocks barely breaking the sea's surface, to large, forested and almost mountainous islands. Barely a single road penetrates the bay's coasts; the only transport links reaching the one and only settlement, El Nido town, which sits at the northern end of the bay in its own very beautiful natural harbour, almost hemmed in by sheer limestone cliffs.

The bay and its islands were originally given protection as a marine reserve in the 1980s in order to protect both local fishing stocks and populations of several species of marine turtle. Since then, the reserve has been greatly expanded to include many of the mainland forests, and it is now known formally as the El Nido-Taytay Managed Resource Protected Area. As a result, the reserve now incorporates an increasingly rare full range of habitats, from open water, through coral reefs and seagrass beds, to sandy beach, beach forest, mangroves, lowland rainforest, and limestone forest.

EL NIDO TOWN

Centre for all the infrastructure and what little action there is, El Nido town lies strung out along a curving shore, with a small jetty to serve supply vessels at its south-west end, the curving beach providing the same facility for the hundreds (really, quite literally) of *bancas* sitting on moorings across the bay. High cliffs press in close to the town's south-west sides, continuing out into the bay, walling the town off from the main expanse of Bacuit Bay and giving almost complete protection from storms.

Above: The beach-cum-harbour at El Nido town, with buildings pushing up to the sands' very edge, backed by sheer cliffs.

Left: Towering rocky and forest-clad hills typify the El Nido landscape, the shoreline itself a mix of rock, tree and sand.

Opposite: A calm dusk over Bacuit Bay and its archipelago, seen from Lagen Island.

Right: The completely sheer coralline limestone cliffs of Lagen Island are typical of many parts of the Bacuit Bay coast.

Opposite: Lagen Island Resort, occupying part of the remote Lagen Island deep inside Bacuit Bay, is one of Palawan's most exclusive places to stay.

Behind the harbour, the town occupies a rare expanse of flat ground, and in recent years has started to run out of space. Improved road, air and ferry links have led to many more people coming to El Nido, as a result of which the town has spilled across to the neighbouring village of Corong Corong. This once quiet fishing settlement now spreads along the beach of the adjoining bay, squeezed between the shore and towering hills.

Today, there are two major concentrations of hotels. The first, and oldest, are El Nido town's original resorts, spread largely along the town beach's north-eastern end and within easy reach of the harbour. The second concentration consists of much newer hotels, spread along the beach in Corong Corong, and some distance from El Nido town's harbour.

THE BACUIT BAY ARCHIPELAGO

An estimated 45 islands lie scattered across Bacuit Bay, creating quite an archipelago, although from El Nido town only one is visible. That is Cadlao Island, the biggest of all the bay's islands, and with a height of 640 m (2,105 ft) by some margin the highest too. It lies to the west of the town, forming a wonderful sunset silhouette dominating the western skyline. The channel that cuts between it and the mainland serves as the gateway to Bacuit Bay and its islands beyond.

Many of the islands are completely ringed by sheer limestone cliffs that plunge straight into the sea from a great height, giving no landing place, while others are lined with wonderful golden sandy beaches, places to play Robinson Crusoe for a while. A few of the larger islands contain good rainforest that can usually be explored, while a handful host some of Southeast Asia's most exclusive resorts, including the Miniloc and Lagen Island Resorts.

There are said to be between 50 and 100 beaches – depending on who you believe – scattered around both the islands and the mainland coasts, not a single one of them accessible by road. A boat is needed to reach every one of them, including the beautiful Seven Commandos Beach, the first of the beaches you reach after leaving El Nido town.

Islands that are easily reached from El Nido town include Dilumacad – nicknamed Helicopter Island, supposedly due to the shape of its outline – long, thin Matinloc, the rugged Tapiutan and the amazingly jagged Miniloc. Lagen and Dolbaduen Islands both lie in the bay's innermost areas, both associated with Lagen Island Resort. Most of these have good beaches and great snorkelling opportunities. Miniloc, in particular, is renowned for the snorkelling in its twin lagoons, two places where sightings of turtles, usually Green or Hawksbill, are almost guaranteed. Close to Miniloc lies Tres Marias, a very jagged three-pointed islet that has become one of El Nido's iconic symbols. There is nowhere to land here, but the islet is surrounded by excellent and very shallow corals, creating a great snorkelling site.

Going deeper, there are some fantastic dive sites in the bay, many of them around Miniloc, Tres Marias, Dilumacad and Cadlao Islands, all offering a diversity of corals and some fantastic fish life that ranges from the small reef fish, such as clownfish, triggerfish and butterflyfish, up to larger, deep-sea species, such as trevally, barracuda and grouper. Several species of ray and turtle are also commonly seen. Sharks are usually encountered only off the outer islands, outside the main enclosure of the bay.

PROTECTING EL NIDO'S WILDLIFE

Though El Nido's marine reserve was set up initially to protect mainly fish stocks and turtles, its expansion to include many of the mainland's forested areas has been hugely important in protecting Palawan's terrestrial wildlife.

The now long-term protection of the marine areas has greatly helped the recovery of corals and the huge diversity of fish species that depend on the reefs, ranging from the tiniest clownfish to the largest ray or grouper. Almost certainly it has also helped the survival of the four species of turtle found here – Hawksbill, Green, Leatherback and Olive Ridley – as well as the very rare Dugong, which frequents shallow seagrass beds rather than the reefs.

On land, the forests are home to all of Palawan's endemic bird species, including the Palawan Hornbill and the Palawan Scops Owl, as well as some that are unique to the Philippines as a whole, such as the Red-vented Cockatoo. All three are now rather rare, largely due to loss of forest habitat, though the last of these also due to the pet trade.

Footpaths do allow some of the forest areas to be explored, and one of the best is on Lagen Island. Despite its small size, there is some rather nice forest here, complete with climbing rattan vines, and a number of Palawan Hornbills. If exploring the more extensive forest areas, particularly on the mainland, always take a guide – the paths are not always that clear and there is no signposting.

In an already beautiful island like Palawan, El Nido is quite certainly one of its prize, jewel locations. It deserves to be protected and cared for far into the future.

Below: Huge buttress roots at the base of a large rainforest tree serve to anchor it in the thin soil of this limestone landscape.

Above: Beach, coconut palms and rainforest on Dolbaduen Island, part of the Lagen Island Resort.

Left: A *banca* lies anchored at Seven Commandos Beach, with a backdrop of Bacuit Bay islands.

PUERTO PRINCESA SUBTERRANEAN RIVER NATIONAL PARK

COASTAL RAINFOREST AND AN UNDERGROUND RIVER

Quite some way south from El Nido, on Palawan's west coast, and just 80 km (50 miles) north of the provincial capital, Puerto Princesa, this is by far the island's most popular visitor attraction.

What everyone comes to see is an underground river, flowing out from a limestone cave and into a lagoon, before crossing a beach and into the sea. The high point of any visit is to take a boat tour up river through the cave, watching out for some of the huge stalactite and stalagmite formations, as well as the flitting and swooping bats and swifts that live here.

Quite apart from this – and something that most visitors do not pay much attention to – is the fact that the underground river is just a relatively minor part of this national park, the protected area's 22,000 ha (54,000 acres) preserving some of Palawan's most important wildlife habitat and hence a huge diversity of both plant and animal species.

THE NATIONAL PARK'S LANDSCAPE

As with El Nido, the landscape is built up primarily from coralline, or karst, limestone, dominated by the enormous dome of Mt St Paul's (1,028 m/3,372 ft), which was given this name in 1850 by British sailors for whom the mountain was reminiscent of London's St Paul's Cathedral. They must have been very homesick, because the resemblance is not particularly striking!

Much of the landscape is covered with limestone rainforest, adapted to the dry, thin soils typical of a limestone environment. There is little surface water: instead rainwater percolates down through the rock and into a vast cave network that creates underground rivers and hence the national park's star attraction. The Cabayagan River flows for just over 8 km (five miles) through the mountain, making it one of the world's longest underground rivers. It also flows on at least two levels within the mountain, creating underground waterfalls that few people have managed to penetrate far enough to see.

A second river, the Poyuy-Poyuy, flows across low-lying ground at the foot of the mountain, entering the sea close to the western edge of the national park. In its final few kilometres it passes through a sprawling mangrove forest, a really quite different forest environment to that of the dry limestone forest a short distance away.

Along the shore, much of which is a sandy beach, there is a narrow band of beach forest, consisting of trees adapted to the dry, sandy and potentially salty conditions typical of the seashore. Offshore, in the sandy shallows are seagrass beds, while further out lies a fringing coral reef that is still in quite good condition. All this comes together to create (as with parts of El Nido) a complete and continuous habitat gradation, starting from a marine coral reef and progressing through the seagrass beds, beach forest and mangroves to terrestrial limestone rainforest, an intactness that is increasingly rare in a world in which natural environments are usually fragmented by human activity.

Right: A tangle of roots marks the shoreline in the dense, primeval mangrove forest lining the Poyuy-Poyuy River, on the western edge of the national park.

WILDLIFE AND ITS CONSERVATION

This one protected area is a treasure trove of species, containing eight of the 13 categories of tropical rainforest identified across the whole of Asia, as well as a third of all the plant species so far identified in Palawan, almost 300 of them trees.

Of the animals, 295 species of vertebrate have so far been found, most of them birds, including all 15 that are endemic, or unique, to Palawan. These include such birds as the Palawan Hornbill, the Palawan Peacock-pheasant and the Tabon Scrub-fowl, the last of these a flightless, chicken-like bird that can sometimes be seen rummaging around in the undergrowth and that incubates its eggs under enormous mounds of soil, sand and leaves.

More easily seen are the very common Long-tailed Macaques and Monitor Lizards, the latter up to about 2 m (6 ft) long, both of which are commonly found around the underground river boat station and the park ranger office.

In recognition of all this biodiversity and the need to protect it, not only is the area a national park, but it has also received a number of international designations. These started as far back as the 1970s when UNESCO gave it the accolade Man and the Biosphere Reserve, followed in the 1990s by World Heritage Site status. More recently, it has become a Ramsar site (that is, a site of global importance for wetland birds), an Important Bird Area and a National Geological Site.

Above: Long-tailed Macaques, also known as Crab-eating Macaques, are common residents of the national park's forest, and are readily seen around the park ranger's station.

Left: Also frequently seen around the ranger station are Monitor Lizards, many up to 2 m (6 ft) long. Though fearsome-looking, they are completely non-aggressive and easy to approach.

Above: The lagoon, completely enclosed by rainforest, into which the subterranean river flows once it leaves the cave and before it crosses the beach and into the sea.

Right and opposite: What visitors can expect to see during a canoe tour along the subterranean river; an eerie place of rock walls, columns and stalactites.

EXPLORING THE NATIONAL PARK

Access from Puerto Princesa is relatively straightforward these days, with a good paved road the whole way to Sabang, the nearest village to the park, and daily tours arranged by hotels and travel companies.

However, the underground river itself has become too popular for just this one single site to cope with, leading the Puerto Princesa city government to control daily numbers, making it compulsory to reserve a place well in advance. Even so, the lagoon shore that serves as the boat dock for tours into the underground river can get quite crowded, so this is rarely the kind of quiet interaction with nature that one might hope for.

Sabang, the entry point to the park, is itself a lovely place, consisting of a vast, coconut palm-lined beach backed by a handful of resorts. The usual route into the park is to take a 10-minute *banca* ride from Sabang's jetty to the park's beach, from where it is barely a five-minute walk to the underground river's boat station. Alternatively, the energetic can hike along a fairly easy path that follows the coast through rainforest, a distance of about 5 km (three miles).

Despite the crowds, the underground river tour is a great experience. Small fleets of tiny outrigger canoes each carrying about 10 passengers travel a kilometre into the cave. No engines are allowed here – the noise and pollution would be awful – so propulsion is via a single oarsman at the stern. The cave is in total darkness, of course, so lighting is via a powerful lamp held and directed by whoever happens to be sitting at the bow. The only sounds come from water dripping from both the oarsman's paddle and the stalactites, combined with the twittering and fluttering of hundreds of bats and swifts. Oh, and of course, the constant commentary from the oarsman.

Beyond the underground river, there are the lagoon, the beach and the rainforest to explore. Monitor Lizards and Long-tailed Macaques are readily seen, while the Tabon Scrub-fowl and the Palawan Hornbill put in occasional appearances. Other bird life may be visible to those that explore the rainforest paths, either that linking the park with Sabang, or the one trail that heads inland into the depths of the park.

Then there are the mangroves of the Poyuy-Poyuy River. Just beyond the Sabang resorts a local community business offers tours through the forest, again in tiny and very quiet, engine-less outrigger canoes that make it possible to hear all the forest's noises, from the constant screaming of the cicadas to the chattering of birds. The mangroves are a deeply primeval place, the trees twisted, gnarled and tangled, draped with layers of moss and hung with lianas. Wildlife is quite difficult to spot, but Long-tailed Macaques can usually be seen, and snakes are a regular feature, resting in some of the trees hanging over the water.

This is a fabulous place, with a lot more to it than just the underground river.

Right: The national park's rainforest is a tangle of vegetation, consisting mostly of quite small trees due to the thin soil and lack of water.

Opposite: A fleet of *bancas* crowds the waterfront at Sabang, waiting for passengers to ferry to and from the national park.

AUSAN'S
AUSAN'S
GENERAL MERCHANDISE
8 Passengers Only
PARK FERRY SERVICE
04-0002338
SABANG

HONDA BAY

DESERT ISLANDS IN A CALM SEA

As desert coral islands go, the 16 uninhabited islands that lie scattered across Honda Bay are just about as good as such islands can get. Consisting of almost pancake-flat strips of ancient coral reef, they are raised just a metre or so above the sea's surface. Most are lined with blindingly white sand, lapped by a shallow, stunningly beautiful azure sea. In some ways, it is possible to see Honda Bay as another El Nido in miniature, only without the mountainous outlines. This comes close to being a tropical paradise.

THE LIE OF THE LAND

With the clear blue water and sky, coupled with the white sand, the light here can be quite harsh and blinding, further enhancing the desert-island mood. Fortunately, most of the islands do have shade, some of the larger ones in particular covered with coconut palms, the beaches lined with small numbers of evergreen trees. In general, these larger islands are not completely ringed by sand, one side usually given over to extensive, vibrantly green mangrove forests.

These pages: Cowrie Island is arguably the most popular of the islands, complete with a welcome sign for the essential selfies.

Below: A beachside tree gives some welcome shade on Cowrie Island.

Opposite: An idyllic beach scene on Cowrie Island.

The waters around the islands are clear and shallow, generating extensive seagrass beds in some of the most sheltered, shallowest waters, home to the occasional very rare and shy Dugong. The slightly deeper waters contain healthy coral reefs very close to shore, providing a home for several turtle species and an array of small reef fish. Since the bay is so shallow, the shoals of deep-sea fish, such as trevally, tuna and barracuda, as well as sharks, seen in many other parts of the Philippines, are just not seen here, but in general this is made up for by the colour and diversity of reef species. It is easy to go snorkelling here – equipment is readily hired – but scuba diving is less common, and is probably best organized in Puerto Princesa.

The shallow water also means that, in the mangrove areas especially, at low tide the water retreats a remarkable distance, opening up vast sand flats that can be larger than the islands themselves. This is a good time to explore the mangroves, walking along their seaward edges to marvel at their fantastic aerial roots, and to spot tiny marine creatures, such as fiddler crabs and mudskippers, scurrying around among the roots and branches. There is bird life here too, especially such shoreline birds as reef egrets and mangrove herons, but also iridescent kingfishers and tiny colourful flowerpeckers.

EXPLORING THE ISLANDS

Lying a short distance north of Puerto Princesa, Palawan's provincial capital, the islands are extremely accessible, meaning that they do become rather busy at weekends and over holidays, but during the week they are quiet, though usually not actually deserted.

Boats out to the islands can be hired at the little village of Santa Lourdes, only just over 10 km (six miles) from the city centre. This is a nice little place in itself, many of the houses strung out along the road leading directly to the wharf, often half hidden and shaded among a tangle of colourful vegetation. This is very much a boating village, many of the houses backing directly onto the shallow waters of the bay's shoreline, *bancas* – some of them remarkably large – in various stages of construction and/or repair squeezed into spaces between trees and houses.

Most people head for any of four islands, most especially Cowrie Island, so named for the huge numbers of cowrie shells that can be found on its beach. With coconut palms covering a large expanse of the island's 'inland' area, there is plenty of shade here, as well as the little archipelago's only cafe, a simple shack that serves up the most delicious, freshest coconuts imaginable.

Other islands include Pandan Island, so named for the large number of pandanus trees that line parts of the beach, Starfish Island, again named after the many starfish to be found in its shallow waters, and finally Snake Island. Thankfully, this is not named after a large snake population but for its long, 'snaking' sandbar that changes its rather wavy, wriggling sort of shape as the tide comes and goes. Snake Island has also recently become a site for a government marine research centre. Finally, there is Lu-li Islet, a shortened form of *lulubog-lilitaw*, meaning that the island goes up and down. In other words, it is not an island at all, but a sandbar that appears above the waves only at low tide.

All but one of the islands are uninhabited. The only one to have any kind of population is Arreciffe Island, the most remote of the Honda Bay Islands, and site of the luxurious Dos Palmas Island Resort. Come here to really escape absolutely everything, except the comforts of life.

AROUND THE BAY

While the islands of Honda Bay are uninhabited, the bay's mainland coast is not, a growing population living along the shore in a string of fishing villages. Not a protected area, Honda Bay's fish populations are under presure, especially as the shoals of deep-sea fish generally remain offshore in deeper water, well away from the shallows of Honda Bay, and so leaving only the much smaller reef fish within easy reach. It is not at all uncommon to find fish traps scattered across many of the mangroves, aiming to snag just any marine life that wanders by. It is to be hoped that conservation measures can maintain the bay's natural environment, while ensuring a sustainable food supply for the local people.

Above right: Coconut palms and beachside, thatched gazebos on Pandan Island.

Right: Low tide reveals vast sandflats that more than double the size of the islands, a great time to explore some of the mangroves that lie along these shores.

Opposite: Visitors return to their *banca* after a day enjoying Pandan Island's beautiful beach.

THE VISAYAS

AN ISLAND LANDSCAPE

When it comes to the Visayas think boat, beach and island, for this is the heart of the Philippines' island landscape, a region divided up into a cluster of seven major islands, a handful of rather lesser ones, and then many hundreds of small and downright tiny islands. Ferry is the usual way to move from island to island, boats ranging from large roll-on-roll-off ships, to fast, sleek catamarans to tiny, traditional *bancas*.

The landscape includes some of the country's busiest cities, places such as Cebu and Iloilo, as well as forested and mountainous volcanoes, such as Mts Talinis and Kanlaon, and many of the Philippines' most spectacular and famous beaches. Paramount among these is of course Boracay, probably the country's number one tourist attraction, but there are also many other great beaches, such as those on Panglao, Malapascua and Siquijor Islands. Associated with many of these beaches are some of the country's best-protected coral reefs, particularly those around Panglao, offering some of the country's best diving.

The Visayan region was among the earliest parts of the Philippines to be taken over by the Spanish, and as a result their cultural remains can be found widely scattered across the islands, mainly in the form of churches, forts and villas. The historic churches are particularly visible, especially in Cebu and Bohol, and although many were badly damaged by an earthquake in 2013, they are slowly being restored.

Anyone who likes island life and island-hopping will love the Visayas.

Left: An early morning, low-tide scene on Boracay's spectacular White Beach; the Philippines' number one tourism attraction.

BORACAY

THE PHILIPPINES' NUMBER ONE TOURIST HOTSPOT

Barely 7 km (4½ miles) long and one kilometre (two-thirds of a mile) wide, this tiny sliver of land lying just off the northern tip of Panay, in the western Visayas, has long held the crown as the Philippines' biggest tourist attraction, the crowds drawn by the strip of blinding white sand, appropriately named White Beach, that runs for nearly 5 km (three miles) along the island's west coast. It is arguably one of the most beautiful beaches in Southeast Asia, backed as it is by stands of swaying coconut palms and lush, green, tropical vegetation, lapped along its shore by a sea of stunning turquoise and aquamarine, making Boracay the quintessential tropical island getaway.

Opposite: A view of just the northern section of Boracay's White Beach and the clear, shallow water that laps its shoreline.

Below: Taking it very easy along the water line on White Beach, with a backdrop of moored *paraw*, traditional sailing outriggers.

FROM BACKWATER TO HOTSPOT

Boracay was first discovered by backpacking travellers in the 1970s and 80s, a time when there was not even any electricity on the island, let alone accommodation. Slowly, over the years simple coconut wood and *nipa* palm lodgings developed along the edge of White Beach, and electricity arrived, as did growing numbers of visitors. By the early 2000s, resorts were scattered along most of the length of the beach, some of them providing a steadily upmarket type of stay. Today, much of White Beach's accommodation is quite exclusive, simple wooden lodgings making way for brash concrete, steel and glass hotels and resorts. Buildings now stretch along the entire length of the beach, though they are still largely hidden among the coconut palms, with shopping malls, restaurants and the occasional scuba-diving operation jostling for space. Those early backpackers are now just a distant memory, replaced by well-heeled holiday-makers and tour groups from all over East Asia, people looking for a relaxing tropical holiday rather than a remote escape.

However, the rapid and rather uncontrolled development that resulted, led in 2018 to the Philippine president forcibly closing the island to all visitors for six months. During that period a major clean-up was conducted, new sewage and drainage systems installed, a number of hotels were ordered to close, and a host of illegal structures were demolished. The island reopened in October 2018, with the promise of a cleaner, more orderly and environmentally friendly Boracay. Of course Covid then forced its closure again a little over a year later, the island only fully reopening to tourism in 2022.

Getting to Boracay has always been something of an adventure. Full-sized jet aircraft bring in visitors from Manila to the airport at the town of Kalibo, about an hour's drive away on the Panay mainland, small aircraft fly into Caticlan on the mainland directly opposite Boracay. *Bancas* and other ferries carry everyone across from Caticlan harbour on the short hop to the island. In days gone by, arrival involved coming ashore on White Beach, new visitors often rather shocked to find that they had to wade through the shallows to reach dry land. With the huge numbers of visitors now arriving, most of them less nimble and less adventurous than the early backpackers, that rather romantic piece of fun has gone, all the ferries now operating from a specially built wharf at Cagban on Boracay's southern tip.

Above: An evening view of a restaurant at Discovery Shores, one of the growing number of upmarket resorts springing up along White Beach.

Left: White Beach is backed by a parallel sandy lane, lined with shops, stalls, cafes and restaurants; a relaxing strip shaded by trees.

Opposite: A beachside scene looking towards Willy's Rock at the far northern end of White Beach.

AROUND THE ISLAND

Although the action is still very much centred on White Beach, many other parts of the island have also been developed. While White Beach faces south-west, a short distance away on the opposite, north-east-facing coast is Bulabog, a shorter beach that is the centre of Boracay's windsurfing, kitesurfing and wakeboarding action. Boards can be hired and lessons taken any time along this beach, and for the competitive and skilled some major international competitions are held here every year, particularly during the north-east monsoon period from October to May, when the wind is onshore.

While Bulabog is generally much quieter than White Beach, during the south-west monsoon, from June to September or October some of the beach action switches to Bulabog due to the rougher seas along White Beach.

On the same side of the island as White Beach and just to the north is Diniwid, a deeply curving bay. Backed by a cliff and cut off from White Beach by a headland that can be walked around at low tide, Diniwid is quite secluded and laidback, a handful of resorts clinging to the steep slopes above the sand.

Moving beyond Diniwid are yet more beaches much smaller, though still stunningly beautiful, and even more secluded, each one today hosting a very small number of upmarket resorts. These include Baling Hai, Punta Bunga and Banyugan Beaches, the last of these now part of a Shangri-La resort. At Boracay's northern tip lies the quiet village of Yapak, site of Puka Beach, an expanse not of sand but of dazzlingly white tiny seashells, utterly beautiful to see. Beyond here, much of the island's north-eastern corner is still quite remote, the beaches up here not as attractive as the jewels along the west coast.

Inland, a large chunk of the northern part of the island is an exclusive golf club and resort, surrounded by some exclusive apartments. It is in this area that still more property development is likely to occur, bringing yet more upmarket accommodation to the island. Further south an entire town has sprung up on the narrow land between White and Bulabog Beaches, servicing not just the visitors but also the army of Filipinos who work on the island.

BENEATH THE WAVES

Boracay is not generally rated among the Philippines' top scuba-diving spots, but actually it is not at all bad, with quite a range of submarine environments to dive into. Most areas are too deep for effective

snorkelling though there are a couple of attractive coral gardens around Crocodile and Laurel Islands, off Boracay's south-eastern tip, and which can be reached by *banca*.

The best of the scuba diving is off the north-west end, particularly on two sites called Yapak 1 and 2, where a sheer wall plunges into deep water, often subject to strong currents. The wall itself is covered in an array of hard and soft corals and barrel sponges, the nooks and crannies of the corals home to quite a number of reef fish. For many divers, however, the big attraction here is the chance to see large deep-sea fish, ranging from sharks to shoals of tuna, jacks and barracuda, that appear out of the deep blue to patrol along the wall in search of food.

Other dive sites along Boracay's west coast are less intense and shallower, but offer wonderful coral scenes and populations of fantastically colourful reef fish, including butterflyfish, surgeonfish, pufferfish and parrotfish.

This underwater environment is like another world, and is really worth exploring. Fortunately, White Beach is well-endowed with diving operations, most of which have been here since Boracay's early days, ensuring a vast amount of experience around the island. For the novice, all of them offer internationally certified diving courses, able to turn any reasonable swimmer into a capable diver in a matter of days.

Above: A cluster of colourful Feather Stars – a starfish that is a very common sight right across the Philippines' coral reefs – makes a home on a rock outcrop off the northern coast of Boracay.

Opposite: Kite-surfing gear lies ready for action – and some wind – along Bulabog Beach, on Boracay's east coast.

IN AND AROUND ILOILO

AN HISTORIC PORT

The fourth largest city in the Philippines, Iloilo is also one of the country's most historic: the site of Spain's second Philippine settlement and the last city in which the Spanish colonial government surrendered to Philippine forces, at the close of the 19th century.

To this day, the city's older districts are marked by remnants of those times past, the district of Jaro to the north of the city home to a Spanish-era cathedral and a smattering of colonial mansions, the downtown area itself site of some fading Hispanic architecture and Plaza Libertad, the very spot where Spanish forces made their surrender. Little remains of the 17th century fort the Spanish built, but their churches still stand strong, not just Jaro Cathedral, but also such places as Molo Church in the western district of that name.

Sitting at the mouth of the Iloilo River, on the south coast of the Visayan island of Panay, Iloilo was an important trade centre long before the Spanish arrived, but is one of the reasons why they took it over during the very early days of their occupation of the country. However, it was an Englishman, Nicholas Loney, the British vice-consul in the city, who helped to make Iloilo wealthy, by creating the sugar-cane industry and ensuring that it was Iloilo's port that shipped the product out. In recent years, the city has struggled a little, something that has shown through in the dour grittiness of many of its downtown streets. Boom times do seem to be returning, however, with the construction of a gleaming new commercial area in the north-western Mandurriao district.

EXPLORING THE CITY

Any tour around the city should start at the Museo Iloilo, a small but well laid out museum that displays artefacts ranging from pre-Hispanic, Chinese and native burial and domestic jars, through religious icons to those indicating the wealth of the 19th century city. From here, head northwards, across the Iloilo River on Forbes Bridge to Jaro to visit the cathedral, its separate belfry and its market – at the foot of the belfry – specializing in locally made ceramic jars. From here, return to the city centre to visit the historic Plaza Libertad and the Spanish-era colonnaded pavements in the adjacent streets, one of the city's main shopping areas.

Next head out west to Molo to see the magnificent 19th century Molo Church – its interior frescoes and whitewashed walls are really quite special – and then take time to relax in the peaceful Molo Plaza, immediately in front of the church. Further west of here is Arevalo, home of Iloilo's weavers. It is often possible to visit them at work in their home studios, where they weave beautiful products on traditional hand looms, using not just cotton but also silk and fibres from plants, such as *pina*, or pineapple, used long before cotton arrived.

Finally, wind up the day by visiting the restaurants along the nearby Villa beach or those in the new Mandurriao shopping district.

Above left and right: The facade and attractive interior of the historic Molo Church, in Iloilo.

Right: Arevalo district is home to the city's weavers, who use traditional hand looms to produce some beautifully patterned cloth.

Opposite: Iloilo's earliest history is represented in the Museo Iloilo by a burial display that includes historic Chinese funerary jars.

THE DINAGYANG FESTIVAL

If there is just one single thing for which today's Iloilo is famed it is the Dinagyang Festival, held annually over the fourth weekend of January. During these few days the city's streets are turned into a series of stages, on which an army of amateur dance troupes perform in fiercely contested competitions.

The festival kicks off on the Friday evening with a huge food event with night markets selling all kinds of meals and snacks lining the street. But it is on Saturday that things seriously get going, with the day-long Kasadyahan dance competition, during which intricately choreographed dances and wonderfully lavish costumes aim to celebrate Iloilo's local life, especially its fishing and farming traditions. On Sunday this is replaced by Ati-atihan, a day during which dances recall a period in the 12th and 13th centuries when Malays immigrating from Borneo were able to settle in Panay as a result of land deals with the local native Aeta people. Cue more lavish choreography and costumes, complete with blackened faces to recall the Aeta, as well as tribal-type costumes and warlike dances. This is a massively spectacular and colourful event, not to be missed.

Above: A lavishly costumed dance troupe goes through its routine during the Ati-Atihan part of Dinagyang Festival, Iloilo's biggest annual party.

Above right: Beautiful Hispanic-type costumes typify the dances performed during the Kasadyahan part of the Dinagyang Festival.

Right: Dinagyang souvenirs are widely available during the festival, such as this Ati-Atihan doll's face, for sale on a street-side stall.

HEADING OUT WEST

A couple of hours' drive west of Iloilo is the town of Miagao, site of one of the Philippines' most spectacular, Spanish-era churches, the Church of Santo Tomas, today a UNESCO World Heritage Site. Completed in 1786, it is built in the usual 'earthquake baroque' style, with thick, buttressed walls intended to resist both earthquake and attack. It is for its magnificent facade that it is justifiably renowned, a series of intricate carvings giving a uniquely tropical interpretation to a European theme, with a coconut tree used to represent the Tree of Life – highly appropriate in a country like the Philippines.

Quite apart from the church, Miagao is a pleasant town to explore, its back alleys home to more skilled weavers, and its beach, though not a fantastic place in terms of the quality of its sand, a great vantage point from which to watch its many fishermen at work on their boats or nets, after the daily catch has been brought in for sale.

Above: The magnificent facade of the 18th-century Church of Santo Thomas, a UNESCO World Heritage Site in the town of Miagao, west of Iloilo. Note the carving of a coconut palm to represent the Tree of Life.

GUIMARAS

THE PHILIPPINES' MANGO CAPITAL

Barely a 15 or 20-minute boat ride away from the bustling city of Iloilo lies the island province of Guimaras, an intensely rural place whose slower, more relaxed rhythms are the complete antithesis to the big city such a short distance away. The city's *banca* ferries come ashore on Guimaras at the small town of Jordan, from where the island's main road leads up through hilly, densely vegetated countryside to San Miguel, the island's very laidback inland provincial capital, before dropping back down to the south-west coast in the area of Nueva Valencia and a scattering of beach resorts.

Much of the island is formed from coralline rock, a massive raised reef that reaches roughly 300 m (1,000 ft) above sea level (with San Miguel sitting near the highest, and hence coolest elevation), resulting in a vegetation able to cope with the dry conditions, as well as a landscape that, during the height of the dry season, can look quite parched.

Along the south-west coast, cliffs of coral rock alternate with occasional sandy coves, extensive mangroves and offshore rocky islands that lend themselves to hidden resort retreats.

On such a rural island, farming is of course the main way of life, and for Guimaras that means growing mangoes. They are by far the main product.

Opposite: The lovely Alubihod Beach, the largest stretch of sand on Guimaras' south-west coast, and the main visitor attraction.

GUIMARAS MANGOES

For many Filipinos the name 'Guimaras' is synonymous with mangoes, there being a widely held belief that the island produces the country's best. It is certainly true that Guimaras produces an awful lot, large parts of the countryside covered with tens of thousands of mango trees, most clearly arranged into neat plantations, but others seemingly distributed randomly across open countryside.

With the trees now bred to bear fruit all year round, stalls permanently line the roads selling mountains of mangoes, both green and yellow, fresh and dried. Anyone wanting to find out more about mango cultivation can wander into the National Mango Research and Development Center at San Miguel, a place to see both orchards of fully mature trees and nurseries filled with seedlings.

It should be said that Guimaras' farmers produce not just mangoes, but also cashews and kapok (whose fluffy seeds are used for stuffing pillows, among other things), though both of these crops seem to be produced mainly from trees growing wild, or semi-wild, in the countryside. Then there are the usual rice and coconut products, though all of these are dwarfed by the mango production.

Left: Piles of mangoes for sale at a roadside stall, one of many that line the main road around San Miguel, a reflection of the importance of this island's crop.

BEACH RESORT

SOUTH-WESTERN COVES

Guimaras does not have the vast expanses of sand that so typify many other parts of the Visayas. What it does have are intimate, and often very secluded coves, virtually cut off – and certainly invisible – from the outside world, many of them on outlying islands or peninsulas separated from the Guimaras mainland by mangrove forests as well as open water.

The main, and most accessible of the beaches is Alubihod, sitting on the northern side of a peninsula on Guimaras' west coast. The few hundred metres of white sand are backed by a string of resorts that are very quiet during the week, but rather crowded and noisy at weekends. It is, nevertheless, a lovely spot and one from which some island- and beach-hopping is possible. There are *bancas* available to head across to Baras Beach, for example, on an opposite headland but inaccessible by road. To the south-west is smaller Guisi Beach, a much quieter and less developed spot, hemmed in by steep forested hills and cliffs. On a nearby headland stands one of Guimaras' few Spanish remains, the ruins of Guisi lighthouse, a once attractive colonial building now picturesquely disintegrating and being reclaimed by the forest. Despite the decay, the site is still in use, the gleaming white modern and hi-tech lighthouse a rather incongruous companion to the historic ruins.

Aside from the beaches, some of the area's mangroves are worth exploring. One of the most accessible areas is just around the headland from Alubihod Beach, protected as part of the John B. Lacson Foundation Marine University Ecological Park. Here an extensive walkway network takes you through dense and very varied mangrove forest, that is home to many of the Philippines' 30-plus species of mangrove tree. Another area where some mangroves can be explored is at Lucmayan, near the island's southern tip. A small harbour here has led to the carving out of small paths through some of the mangroves, and this is the starting point for boats travelling out to the hidden Cabugan Adventure Resort.

OTHER ISLAND SIGHTS

Where there are neither mangroves nor beaches, rocky coralline coves create harbours for fishing boats, one of the most extensive and picturesque of which is at the hamlet of Magamay, between Guisi and Alubihod.

Around on Guimaras' eastern side much of the coast consists of low-lying coralline rock shores, devoid of coves, beaches and mangroves, so points of interest divert inland. These include one very traditional sight: salt farms that access sea water from wells beneath the ground, and which then drive the water off in evaporation ponds. At the other end of the tradition and technology scale, parts of the San Lorenzo area are now given over to a very new wind farm whose vast, power-generating turbines spread across a large area of countryside. While some may dispute their attractiveness, they have certainly made a huge difference to Guimaras' power supply situation, and have enabled at least some farmers to earn a ground rental income.

Above: The harbour and protected bay at Magamay, on Guimaras' south-west coast, lined with the posts and nets of countless fish traps and farms.

Opposite: A coralline limestone outcrop at Guisi Beach, a typical feature of Guimaras' coastline.

CEBU CITY AND MACTAN ISLAND

CAPITAL OF THE VISAYAS

The Philippines' second city may be rather small in comparison to Manila, but it is still a major conurbation sprawling along Cebu's east coast, its tentacles spreading over into adjacent Mactan Island. This is the commercial and industrial hub of the Visayas, and it has been this way for many hundreds of years. When Ferdinand Magellan made landfall here in 1521, followed some 34 years later by Miguel Lopez de Legazpi, the man who really started the Spanish takeover of the Philippines, Cebu was already the business heart of the archipelago, a meeting point for Chinese, Arab and Southeast Asian traders.

That commercial tradition continues to this day, and although the Spanish have long gone, some of their relics remain, creating points of interest for visitors. Most of the city's tourism is concentrated over on Mactan Island, historically the site of Magellan's death at the hands of local chief Lapu Lapu – now lauded as the Philippines' first patriot. Today, the island hosts Cebu's airport and a string of resort hotels that line its east coast.

NAVIGATING THE CITY

Cebu's port stretches along the coast mainly to the south of Mactan Island, with the old part of the city, called Downtown, clustered nearby. The sprawling modern city – known as Uptown – is a couple of kilometres inland and connected to Downtown via the arrow-straight President Osmeña Boulevard. For crowded markets and remnants of the Spanish era head for Downtown. For hotels, restaurants and massive shopping malls, Uptown is the place to be.

The number one attraction is without doubt the Basilica Minore del Santo Niño, a church originally established in 1565 to house a small statue of the Santo Niño, Christ as a child, brought to Cebu by Magellan. The present church dates from the 18th century, and is pretty much in its original form, apart from the belfry. That came crashing down in the 2013 earthquake, but a gleaming white replica now stands in its place. This particular Santo Niño statue is revered across the Philippines, so the church is a major destination for pilgrims.

Straight across the road from the Basilica is the much quieter Metropolitan Cathedral, an elegant 19th century building, while a few streets away is Magellan's Cross, a small rotunda housing a replica of the one Magellan is believed to have planted in the ground here following his arrival. It is said that inside the cross are fragments of the original. The rotunda's ceiling shows paintings depicting the imagined scene: Magellan's men planting the cross watched over by Magellan himself and a priest, along with a crowd of his soldiers and some slightly bemused locals.

The collection of Spanish remnants is rounded off by the nearby Fort San Pedro, built in 1565 and believed to be the oldest surviving Spanish building in the Philippines. It remains quite intact, and today is a pleasant, leafy walled garden worth exploring and relaxing in.

There is not much by way of specific tourist attractions in modern Uptown, unless you count the vast shopping mall that is the Ayala Center, but out in the hilly western suburbs one place to visit is the Philippine Taoist Temple, a huge construction that climbs the steep sides of a hill. Not only is it a place of classical Chinese fanciful architecture, with its bright colours, lanterns and writhing dragons, but it also has a great view across parts of the city.

Above: A writhing dragon and sweeping roof eaves characterize the architecture of the Philippine Taoist Temple, in Cebu City's western suburbs.

Left: Magellan's Cross and the ceiling of the rotunda housing it, recall the 1521 arrival in Cebu of Ferdinand Magellan, the very beginning of Spain's presence in the Philippines.

Opposite: The facade of the Basilica Minore del Santo Nino, complete with its new post-earthquake belfry, home to a very small but highly revered 16th-century statue of Jesus as a child, making this the Visaya's most important religious centre.

BANTAYAN ISLAND

THE EASY-GOING BEACH SCENE

Off the north-western tip of Cebu island, less than 150 km (93 miles) away from the crowds of Cebu City, sits Bantayan Island, the largest in an island cluster. Just 16 km long (10 miles) and reachable only by slow ferries from the port of Hagnaya, on the Cebu mainland, Bantayan is very much at the end of the line, as far as Cebu goes, and the pace and style of life here reflect that. As a largely rural island with a simple road network and just two towns, Santa Fe and Bantayan Town, the latter the administrative capital, there is really not a great deal to be in a hurry about here.

The reason to visit, however, is the stunning, blinding white sand beach that stretches along the island's south-east coast at Santa Fe, a place that is slowly attracting a growing trickle of visitors. They come here to escape the urban rat race, to relax in the joy of a beach whose main selling card is that there is just nothing to do. Don't come here if you need noisy nightclubs and raucous parties!

SANTA FE AND ITS BEACHES

Santa Fe is the main arrival point for ferries coming from the Cebu mainland, so there really is not very far to go to reach a resort after getting off the boat. Hence, the introduction to Bantayan is Santa Fe's long, long jetty at which tie up a motley collection of rusting old ships, delivering or taking away an assortment of freight.

It can seem like a long, hot walk down that jetty, but once you reach land a veritable jungle of coconut palms creates plenty of shade. Here you have a choice of turning right or left, north or south, beaches stretching along the coast on both sides of the jetty, Alice Beach to the north, Sugar Beach to the south. It could be argued that the latter is the main beach, as it is down this way that the town of Santa Fe itself sits, about 2 km (1¼ miles) south of the jetty, but resorts are strung out along the length of both beaches. Just about all the resorts are small and relatively simple, owned and run largely by local people, or at least by entrepreneurs from no further afield than Cebu. There are no huge international resort complexes here, not yet anyway.

Opposite: Alice Beach is an enticing strip of coconut palm-lined sand stretching along Bantayan's south-east coast, to the north of Santa Fe's long jetty.

Below: Santa Fe's jetty lies at the heart of the town's business life, and is a busy place when ferries arrive from the Cebu mainland.

The town is a simple but spacious grid of dusty streets, lined largely with rather non-descript concrete buildings, populated by some of the most relaxed and friendly people you could ever hope to meet. Many of the houses are softened by veritable forests of engulfing vegetation, gardens bursting with multi-coloured plantlife that ranges from banana, papaya and frangipani trees to bougainvilleas, hibiscus and orchids. Here and there a few wooden houses remain, decorated with delicate and elegant fretwork and carvings; dilapidated, rotting, unloved and uncared for, abandoned in the rush for concrete and the drive to modernize.

On the edge of town stand the similarly disintegrating ruins of a Spanish fort, almost completely lost among vegetation, but still standing close to the beach and right in the island's south-easternmost corner. This is just where the coast does a sharp turn, abruptly changing from running north-south to being almost east-west. It is also in this area that you will find most of the restaurants and beach cafes catering to the visitors, a cluster of attractive restaurants lining some of the town's final streets shortly before they run into the sand.

Close by, out on the sand itself but still shaded by clusters of coconut palms, a growing gaggle of basic bars and cafes attracts a steadily increasing number of thirsty sunbathers, exhausted by the exertion of enjoying the view.

Above: Most of Santa Fe's buildings are bland concrete, but a few old wooden buildings survive, decorated with attractive fretwork and carvings, but sadly all are uncared for and in a state of collapse.

Top: Santa Fe's main stretch of sand, Sugar Beach, is lined with a string of small attractive resorts, such as Hoyohoy Villas, one of the most attractive.

THE FINEST SAND

The beach itself consists of some of the finest and most dazzlingly white coral sand that you'll find anywhere in the Philippines, stretching about 4 km (2½ miles) along Santa Fe's south-eastern shore, the town's jetty the only significant interruption. At high tide the beach is rather narrow, but when the waters withdraw they reveal to the south a magnificent sand bar, separated from the main shore by a narrow, shallow lagoon, that is definitely worth exploring. For those who need something a bit more energetic, it is possible to hire bicycles and motorbikes to head out into the island's lovely green countryside. For those who like to go beneath the waves, with no dive operation alas there seem to be few opportunities. However, it is possible to hire a *banca* for snorkelling trips to some of the nearby minor islands, where coral is supposedly more abundant than it is around Bantayan.

When you've done all that there really is very little else to do except to relax, unwind and enjoy the peace and slow pace of Bantayan's life. And, of course, quench one's thirst in one of those beach bars.

Above: The quintessential tropical island beach, the beautiful sand bar and lagoon that appear along Sugar Beach at low tide.

Right: Bantayan Island's south-east corner, close to Santa Fe's centre, is a cluster of beach bars, catering to the growing number of visitors.

MALAPASCUA ISLAND

FROM REMOTE FISHING VILLAGE TO INTERNATIONAL BEACH DESTINATION

Lying a few kilometres off Cebu's northernmost tip, Malapascua is a gem of an island, barely 2.5 km long and 1 km wide (one-and-a-half by two-thirds of a mile), some of its shores lined with fine white sand. In little more than a decade, it has gone from an obscure, impoverished island of fishermen to one of the Philippines' growing band of internationally renowned beach resorts. As with many similar places, the island was first 'discovered' by a few intrepid travellers, most attracted by reports of great diving, and in particular an almost assured opportunity to see significant numbers of the normally elusive Thresher Shark.

THE BEACH LIFE

Reached from the Cebu mainland by *banca* ferry from the harbour village of Maya, there is no way to take a vehicle to Malapascua, which is just as well because the island has no roads. There is a handful of villages, the main one called Logon, sitting in the island's south-west corner. A network of dusty, sandy paths criss-cross the island, linking up the settlements, and although there is no signposting on such a small island it is quite hard to get lost for very long.

The island sits at the junction of the Visayan and Camotes Seas, and so on the map may look rather exposed. However, it is generally well protected from typhoons by the huge bulk of Leyte lying a relatively short distance to the east, though that did not prevent Malapascua from taking quite a pounding in November 2013 from Typhoon Yolanda (known internationally as Typhoon Haiyan), said to have been one of the strongest ever recorded. Some very significant damage was inflicted on the island's buildings, but that was quickly repaired, and Malapascua's life was soon back to normal.

Most of Malapascua's resorts line the beautiful 1-km (⅔-mile) long Bounty Beach, taking up pretty well the whole of the island's south coast. While this now adds up to quite a number of resorts, development has remained low-key and mostly in tune and in harmony with the beauty of the beach and the coconut palms under which the buildings nestle. The result is a relaxed atmosphere along the whole beach, even at busy times.

Some of the resorts have been on Malapascua since the very beginning of its tourism rise, most especially Cocobana and Malapascua

Above: Malapascua's boat-lined, palm-shaded Bounty Beach at the end of the day, seen in evening sunlight just before sunset.

Left: A *banca* from the Malapascua Exotic Island Dive Resort prepares to take a group of divers out to one of the nearby reefs.

Opposite: Life's a beach; a beachside bar spreads out onto the sand on Bounty Beach.

Exotic Island Resort, both with prominent positions on Bounty Beach. The latter was the first to launch the island's diving facilities and to discover the thresher shark phenomenon. Today, of course, many of the resorts have dive centres, offering dives not only to see the sharks – which congregate on nearby Monad Shoal, where manta rays can also sometimes be seen – but also to a number of local coral reefs. Dive sites lie scattered around the island's shores as well as a number of offshore islets and rocks, almost guaranteeing some great diving.

EXPLORING THE ISLAND

With the resorts concentrated at the southern end of the island, much of Malapascua remains barely touched by tourism. Its inland areas are a mix of scrubby vegetation and grazing land, with a few fishing settlements scattered along the shores. The entire island can be walked around in a few hours, but it is best to start out very early in the morning when the air is nice and cool.

The west coast starts off with Logon, the island's main village, a crowded cluster of houses and a few shops, pressed together along the shore of a sheltered, curving bay, then continues to the north with a couple of enclosed bays that house boat-repair areas. In the north-west, an automated lighthouse sits atop one of Malapascua's few hills, from the top of which is a good view across the north-west coast and the village of Guimbitayan. Beyond here, the north coast consists of a spectacular white sand beach, still largely unspoiled, the preserve of local fishermen and the little village of Longob.

This fabulous stretch of sand is followed in the north-east by a couple of small, almost concealed coves, but from there on much of the east coast is lined with coral rocks and is difficult to reach due to dense vegetation. A direct track leads past this area, eventually connecting up with a network of paths that cut through the coconut groves of the island's south and leading back to Bounty Beach.

Even more so than Bantayan, with no roads, no traffic and also no mains electricity – power comes from a few generators – Malapascua is a world away from the modern, bustling metropolis of Cebu City, and yet the two are separated by less than 140 km (87 miles) of road and sea. So leave your phones, laptops and tablets at home: come here to escape all that.

Above: The beachside restaurant at the Malapascua Exotic Island Dive Resort, one of the earliest resorts to have been established on Malapascua.

Right: The beautiful beach at Longob, on Malapascua's north coast, is still the preserve of fishermen.

IN AND AROUND DUMAGUETE

BETWEEN SEA AND MOUNTAIN

Sitting on the south-east coast of the island of Negros, in the heart of the Visayas, Dumaguete is rather blessed. Not only does it have a wonderful location on a relatively sheltered coast, backed by rugged Mt Talinis, but also it is quite atypical of Philippine provincial cities, having a rather cosmopolitan and outward-looking mood, engendered by the presence of Silliman University, one of the country's most well-known seats of learning.

That said, for a visitor, although the city makes for an enjoyable base, it is the surrounding area that is the main attraction, ranging from the dolphins and whales in nearby Tanon Strait, separating Negros from Cebu, to the forests, waterfalls and lakes on the slopes of Mt Talinis. Dumaguete is, you might say, something of an eco-tourism centre.

EXPLORING THE CITY

The city has a pleasant relaxed ambience to it, along with an air of urban sophistication lent to it by the university and the large numbers of foreign students who call this home. The city centre itself consists of a relatively small but spacious grid of streets, some lined with old art-deco buildings, a short distance from the seafront and its attractive promenade. At the hub of the city centre are the lively and colourful central market and Dumaguete Cathedral, the latter fronting onto the plaza that is Quezon Park.

The cathedral dates from the 19th century, though its facade is an interesting early 20th century addition, complete with rather incongruous Greco-Roman column statues of four of the Apostles. Nearby stands the Bell Tower, all that remains of a much older and long-lost cathedral, and Dumaguete's only genuinely old historical monument.

Much of Silliman University, set up in the early days of the USA's colonial rule of the Philippines and the first private American university in Asia, is integrated into the city. Many of the university's older buildings are concentrated in the area between the port and the city centre, along with several attractive, tree-lined avenues. The most prominent of the buildings is the wooden Silliman Hall, built in 1909, and said to be the oldest building in the Philippines constructed in the American 'Eastern Stick' style. Today, it houses the university's Anthropology Museum.

Silliman Hall sits at a busy street corner, at the northern end of Dumaguete's seafront promenade. By day, the promenade is a little non-descript, but at night it comes alive as many of the bars and restaurants lining the seafront road spread out onto the street, turning it into a huge al fresco restaurant area.

To the north of the city centre lies another university site, the Center for Tropical Conservation Studies, usually abbreviated to just Centrop. Resembling simply a small zoo, it is intended to be a captive-breeding project for a number of highly endangered Philippine animals, principally the Philippine Spotted Deer and the Visayan Warty Pig, both of which are unique to Philippine rainforests and which would be almost impossible to see in the wild. Although the animals are not kept in particularly pleasant conditions – the Center is clearly struggling to function on very limited funds – it is worth dropping by to see these rare animals, and of course to make one's own small contribution.

Right: The early 20th-century facade of Dumaguete Cathedral, complete with two of the rather incongruous Greco-Roman style statues of the Four Apostles.

DOLPHIN-WATCHING

Dolphin-watching in the Tanon Strait is one of the area's main draw-cards. Separating Negros from Cebu to the east, the strait is immensely deep – well over 500 m (1,640 ft) in fact – and its waters attract large numbers of whales and dolphins. Although there are said to be 11 species of cetaceans living in the strait, visitors are most likely to see just two species, Risso's and Spinner Dolphins. Whales can be seen from time to time, though their presence is relatively unreliable and usually consists of only the smaller species, such as pilot whales.

Dolphin-watching trips operate mainly out of the town of Bais, about an hour's drive north of Dumaguete, and from the village of Manjuyod, a little further north again. Early morning is the best time of day to go, when calm, windless conditions make it much easier to spot even distant schools of dolphins. Sightings of and interaction with several groups are almost certain, and although the Risso's Dolphins tend to be rather shy and may dive when a boat comes too close, the Spinner Dolphins seem to relish riding along under a boat's bow, frequently leaping clear of the water. Watching these amazing animals can be an exciting, exhilarating experience.

Moreover, despite the Tanon Strait's immensely deep waters, offshore from Manjuyod lies a sandbar that is exposed at low tide, making a great place for a picnic and a swim. Several stilted bungalows have been built here, available for hire, making it possible to stay over even at high tide, when the bar is covered.

Above: Visitors standing in the bow of a *banca* get a chance to photograph dolphins skipping along a calm sea just ahead of the boat.

Below: Spinner Dolphins are a very common sight in the Tanon Strait, a deep stretch of water separating the Visayan islands of Negros and Cebu.

FORESTS AND LAKES

Inland and just north of Dumaguete, nestling on the north-east slopes of Mt Talinis, is the Balinsasayao Twin Lakes Natural Park, a protected area that encloses much of southern Negros' last remaining stretches of primary tropical rainforest, as well as Lakes Balinsasayao and Danao, both ancient volcanic craters.

A winding, bumpy road leads from the coastal village of Sibulan to the park gate, which stands just alongside a third and much smaller lake, Kabalin-an. From here, the forest starts to close in. There is a small amount of swamp forest growing in the shallows of this lake, and the main forest, complete with large dipterocarp trees – the real giants of the lowland rainforest – starts on the lake's far shores. The road eventually climbs up through forest to a cafe and a viewpoint above Lake Balinsasayao, at a cool, refreshing altitude of 900 m (2,900 ft), the lake completely surrounded by forest-clad mountain peaks.

Boats can be hired for a bit of lake paddling, while a number of trails head off into the forest for those in need of some hiking. There is, alas, not much chance of seeing any of those endangered deer or pigs in this forest, though there are some here, but the area is renowned for its bird life, including a number of species that are endemic, or unique, to the Philippines. Come very early or late in the day to maximize chances of seeing plenty of bird life.

THE SOUTHERN SLOPES OF MT TALINIS

Also known as the Cuernos de Negros, the Horns of Negros, in reference to its twin peaks, the highest of which reaches 1,870 m (6,134 ft), Mt Talinis dominates the landscape around Dumaguete. It is possible to hike to the summits, along a number of trails that head out from the town of Valencia, a few kilometres south-west of Dumaguete. The trip up and back can be done in a single day, though the route is steep and sweaty, and there isn't much of a view – most of the route is enclosed, initially by coconut palms, and later surrounded by dense forest, a canopy of trees and an understorey of rattans, pandans, gingers and ferns, among many other plants.

The area is also known for its lovely waterfalls, the most spectacular of which is Casaroro Falls, a sheer 30-m (98-ft) cascade that plunges down a cliff, with a river flowing away from it in a deep canyon enveloped in forest. It is not that easy to reach, a just-motorable track eventually giving way to a 300 plus-step descent into the canyon, followed by a hike up-river over boulders to a viewpoint at a bend in the river. Do not even think about trying to swim in the pool at the waterfall's base – the force of the falling water is far too great.

Previous pages: A stunning view across farmland around the town of Siaton northwards to the Mt Talinis range.

Above: Densely forested mountain slopes form a backdrop to Lake Balinsasayao, in the heart of Balinsasayao Twin Lakes Natural Park, north-east of Dumaguete.

Left: The magnificent Casaroro Falls is arguably the most spectacular waterfall near Dumaguete, pouring down the southern slopes of Mt Talinis, near the town of Valencia, south-west of Dumaguete.

Opposite: Rainforest crowds around the shore of Kabalin-an Lake, on the edge of Balinsasayao Twin Lakes Natural Park.

SIQUIJOR

THE TRANQUIL ISLAND

Need somewhere to fall out of the rat race, where you can just lie in the sand or lounge around in a bar and there will be no-one telling you that you must get on with this job or take that tour? Siquijor is the place for you then.

A CORAL ISLAND

A single, roughly triangular island that is the Philippines' third smallest province, it is a wholly rural place, even its principal centres, Larena and Siquijor town little more than sprawling villages. Unlike much of the Philippines, the island does not rear up into rugged mountains, but rises in a gently sloping hump that culminates in Mt Malabohoc, the island's highest point at 628 m (2,060 ft). Siquijor is no seething volcano but a massive, and massively raised, coral reef. Even up in the inland hills sea shells remain strewn around the soil.

Its seashore remains wholly coralline, and reefs – not pristine but still in good condition, if rather heavily fished – lie offshore along much of the coast. White sandy beaches alternate with low coral cliffs and the occasional mangrove forest, all lapped by a sea that for much of the year is very placid indeed.

Villages lies scattered along the coast and up into the inland hills, but nowhere is the population high, and agriculture is on quite a small scale, taking up mostly the coastal plains. Much of the landscape is very green, the coast planted with the ubiquitous coconut palm, the hills still largely covered with forest, albeit a rather scrubby variety that is able to thrive on the dry, porous, coralline limestone base rock. As with most limestone areas, the hills are riddled with caves, and although rivers are rather few, a number of streams do come to the surface, producing a couple of stunning waterfalls.

One phenomenon that sadly is no longer visible was first described by early Spanish invaders, who arrived in the second half of the 16th century. They called Siquijor *Isla del Fuego*, the Island of Fire, an odd name for a place with not a single volcano. Apparently, they named it so after the eerie glow the island emitted at night, the result of a vast number of fireflies! Siquijor still has fireflies, of course, but alas not on that scale!

MYSTERY AND MAGIC

The people of Siquijor are one of the few Philippine groups outside of the high mountains of northern Luzon to have retained some of their pre-Hispanic pre-Christian practices, specifically an extensive use of herbal remedies and spells to treat a whole host of ailments in a style that has been compared with shamanism. Today, only a few practitioners remain, almost entirely women and mostly now very old. Throughout the rest of the Philippines this has given Siquijor a reputation as a place of mystery, magic, witchcraft and witches, which over the years has served to keep outsiders away for fear of the effects of the island's perceived evil spirits.

That is still partly true today, though there is a slowly growing, more positive interest, helped by efforts to raise Siquijor's tourism appeal, along with an annual festival held on the island every Easter to celebrate not only its own traditional healers but also those from across the Philippines.

SIQUIJOR'S BEACHES

Though just a relatively short ferry ride away from the city of Dumaguete, on Negros, Siquijor remains firmly off the beaten track, at least in part due to its reputation for mystery and magic, though that situation in itself of course creates the perfect environment for an escape from the crowds. The island's main attractions are its beaches, in particular the long strip of blindingly white, coconut palm overhung sand along the south coast, centred around the friendly village of San Juan. This is where most of the island's resorts are to be found, all still rather small and locally owned, but all the nicer for that. One of the great attractions of the San Juan beach is that there is really almost nothing to do here, except relax and enjoy the view.

For those who have to be active, there are several dive centres, mostly along the beach at San Juan. Here, the original dive operation (and hence the most experienced) is Last Frontier, which specialises in taking only very small groups of divers. What they do not know about Siquijor's reefs is probably not worth knowing!

Above: A line-up of tricycles waiting for passengers; the universal way to get around on Siquijor, if not across much of rural Philippines.

Opposite: Sand, palms and a thatched cottage, a classic scene along the beach at San Juan, on Siquijor's south coast.

There are other nearby beaches to explore, most notably Paliton, a few kilometres west of San Juan. Some way off the main road and with access across private land, the beach remains remarkably secluded and free of any tourism development, despite being one of Siquijor's most beautiful scenes. Paliton firmly remains a place for fishermen, its tall palms sheltering lines of fishing boats and tackle, at its western end a small shop where freshly caught fish are bought and sold.

Siquijor's other main concentration of beach resorts lies at Sandugan, close to the island's northernmost tip. Even quieter than San Juan, the Sandugan resorts lie several kilometres from Larena, the nearest town, each one lost among trees and farmland, clinging to a sloping coral cliff and overlooking a lovely white sand beach. A few mangroves fringe the edges of this beach, but for a real mangrove forest it is best to head to Cuiwanon Spring Park, on the edge of Larena town. There, raised boardwalks have been built out across an extensive mangrove area, providing a rare opportunity to really explore just what a mangrove forest looks like, even at high tide.

Right: Raised boardwalks make for easy exploration of the mangrove forest at Cuiwanon Spring Park, on the edge of Larena, Siquijor's largest town.

Below right: A fisherman on Paliton beach with the morning's catch.

Opposite: The stunning beach at Paliton, just west of San Juan, on the south coast.

Below: A low-tide view of the sands at Sandugan, another of Siquijor's beach areas, on the island's north coast.

EXPLORING A BIT OF HISTORY

Travelling eastwards along the coast from San Juan, you first come to the Balete tree, a huge and beautiful banyan, said to be about 400 years old, its vast buttresses and tangles of aerial roots reaching down to the ground and shading a lovely clear spring pool, a place to freshen up. Beyond this lies the town of Lazi, site of Siquijor's most important historical site: the San Isidro Labrador Church, built by the Spanish in the latter half of the 19th century. Not only is this church really quite large and in unusually good condition, but also across the road and shaded by huge acacia trees is the Philippines' oldest convent, a lovely – if now sadly decrepit – colonial building that today houses a school and a museum.

In a similar vein, in Siquijor town stands another Spanish-era chuch, the Church of St Francis of Assisi, much smaller than San Isidro and in a poorer state of repair, but interesting nonetheless for having a bell tower that is quite separate from the main church building.

HEADING INLAND

Heading up into the hills it is possible to explore some very remote rural scenery, a scattering of hamlets and a few great viewpoints across to Negros, with Mt Talinis towering over Dumaguete. There are caves to be explored high up in the hills, as well as a nature park, but more accessible from the coast are a couple of lovely waterfalls. Just inland from Lazi are Cambugahay Falls, where the water has a lovely blue colour, descending down several steps along a relatively gentle slope, and with several very popular swimming holes. Inland from San Juan are Lugnason Falls, a much steeper place, with a vertical drop over a short cliff, the entire waterfall enveloped in dense, steeply sloping forest.

Above right: The 400-year-old Balete tree, shading a small pool, beside the road between San Juan and Lazi.

Right: The San Isidro Labrador Church is one of Siquijor's most historic Spanish relics, standing on the edge of Lazi, on the island's south coast.

Above: A small section of the lovely Cambugahay Falls, complete with swimming hole, in the hills above Lazi.

Left: The more rugged Lugnason Falls, cascading down steep slopes and enveloped in forest close to San Juan.

BOHOL

CORAL REEFS, HISTORIC CHURCHES AND CHOCOLATE HILLS

Just a short distance east of Cebu, the island province of Bohol is something of a Philippines in miniature. Its landscapes offer a taste of just about everything available across the rest of the country, ranging from stunning coral reefs and white sand beaches along the coast, to slow-moving rivers, waterfalls, dense rainforests, rugged hills and some interesting and unique wildlife. Some of its hilly farmlands can even offer up a few rice terraces, while the towns and villages host quite a collection of historic, Spanish-era churches. Some of the latter were, alas, seriously damaged by the 2013 earthquake, which devastated large parts of Bohol, though some progress has been made with restoration work since then.

Bohol's most iconic landscape is without doubt the Chocolate Hills, an area of unique rounded hillocks, whose shrivelling vegetation turns the hills rather brown towards the end of the dry season. Lying almost in the centre of the island, this slightly strange scene has been used to promote the Philippines as a whole through hundreds of posters, advertisements and websites over the years, suggesting rather oddly

that this is the quintessential Philippine landscape. In fact, although the Chocolate Hills are generally a 'must-see' item on every visitor's itinerary, Bohol's main attraction is the island of Panglao, lying just off the south-west coast.

PANGLAO ISLAND

Connected to the Bohol mainland via two bridges just south of Tagbilaran, the provincial capital, Panglao attracts visitors for its white sand beaches, which line much of its coastline. Some are restricted mainly for use by a few exclusive resorts, so the most popular public beach is Alona, in Panglao's south-west. Originally made popular in the 1980s and 90s by divers drawn by the superb coral reefs around Panglao, today it attracts a good many general visitors. As a result, the beach is becoming increasingly busy, with ever larger and more upmarket resorts crowding the shoreline. Despite this, it is still a pleasant and relaxing place, and as a base from which to go diving or to explore the rest of Bohol it is hard to beat.

Alona Beach is at the hub of one of the Philippines' prime diving areas, with quite a collection of dive sites spread around both Panglao's shores and those of several off-lying islands. The diving starts with the house reef less than 100 m (325 ft) off the beach, site of a good diversity of hard and soft corals, as well as some colourful species of reef fish. The star attraction, however, is Balicasag Island, a pancake-flat coral island 6 km (4 miles) to the south-west. As if Balicasag's spectacular white sand beach were not enough, it is also surrounded by fantastic coral reefs and a sheer wall that have been protected as a marine reserve since the 1980s. As a result, they are home to a hugely diverse and healthy population of corals, sponges, anemones and reef fish. The deep waters all around the island also ensure a regular supply of shoals of pelagic fish, trevally, jacks and barracuda regularly seen, along with the occasional shark.

Above: A tree stump lies washed up on the deserted beach that encircles beautiful Balicasag Island.

Opposite top: A plethora of trinkets for sale at a stall on Alona Beach, including sharks' teeth, cowries and other sea shells.

Opposite bottom: Alona Beach is the main attraction for visitors on Panglao Island's south coast.

Right: Two hard corals growing cheek-by-jowl on one of the steep slopes that characterize the underwater world around Balicasag Island.

Below: A Green Turtle – a common sight around many of the Philippines' coral reefs – attempts to demolish a coral growing close to Balicasag Island's shore.

Other good dive sites to the south-east of Alona include those around Pamilacan Island and Cervera Shoal, the latter a shallow sandy area that is home to large numbers of sea snakes. It is in this area too, and particularly between Pamilacan and Balicasag, that schools of dolphins are a regular sight. Early morning boat trips out from Alona and Pamilacan will regularly yield sightings of several groups.

Although most of Panglao's attractions lie along the coast, inland a few places are worth visiting. A few kilometres east of Alona is Tarsier Botanika, a wonderful tropical garden, complete with ponds, some very Thai-looking Buddha statues and an attractive restaurant with great sea views. At Panglao's far eastern end, the village of Dauis has one of Bohol's most historic churches, the Church of our Lady of the Assumption. Decorated with beautiful ceiling paintings, the church was damaged by the 2013 earthquake, but it did survive and has been repaired.

THE COAST OF MAINLAND BOHOL

The mainland's only beach resort area is at Anda, in Bohol's far south-east. Here, the main beach is centred on the town of Anda itself, though resorts are strung out for several kilometres along the coast, mostly on raised coral cliffs, with a variable, though mostly sandy beach below. Due to the coralline limestone nature of the landscape, the area is riddled with caves. Some of these are filled with swimming holes, while others house prehistoric cave paintings that have earned the Anda region a reputation as the cradle of Boholano civilization.

Top: The lovely lush garden at Tariser Botanika is a green and colourful tropical haven, just east of Alona Beach.

Above: The coralline limestone landscape around Anda, on Bohol's south-east coast, is riddled with caves and flooded sinkholes that create great natural swimming pools.

Right: Logarita Pool, a natural spring pool near the inland town of Bilar, and on the edge of Rajah Sikatuna Protected Landscape, is a very popular place for the locals to cool off.

Below right: Floating restaurants catering to large tour groups make regular trips up the Loboc River, starting and finishing at the town of Loboc.

FORESTS, HILLS AND RIVERS

Inland Bohol is intensely rural, a patchwork of farmland and forests, hills and plains. The primary visitor attraction is, as mentioned above, the Chocolate Hills, lying just south of the town of Carmen. Almost all of Bohol's visitors converge on the one principal viewpoint, making it quite a busy place and one bedecked with cafes and souvenir stalls, though the view across these strange hills is quite stunning, particularly in the golden sunlight shortly before sunset.

Between here and the south coast lie a string of places worth visiting, the most southerly of which is the pleasant little town of Loboc, sitting on the banks of the Loboc River. This is the start and finish point for boat tours upriver through a lush, green landscape, a mix of forest and coconut groves crowding in beside the river. The trips are designed to cater for large tour groups, so they can be rather crowded, noisy affairs, complete with constant loud music, but at least the scenery is lovely.

Further north, near the town of Bilar is Logarita Pool, a very refreshing swimming pool created from three natural springs. Close by is the entrance to Rajah Sikatuna Protected Landscape, named after the Boholano chieftain who, in 1565 signed a blood compact with the Spanish conquistador Miguel Lopez de Legaspi. This 9,000-ha (22,300-acre) protected area is one of the last remaining blocks of genuinely primary (i.e. untouched) rainforest in Bohol. A beautiful place that can be explored via a network of trails, this is a well known bird-watching area due to the high diversity of bird species found here, including a number of endangered endemics. This is also home to a number of mammals, including Long-tailed Macaques, flying lemurs, civets and the much-loved Philippine Tarsier. With a body that is just 5 cm

(2 inches) long, this is the world's smallest primate, one of only four species of tarsier in the world, and restricted to just the southern half of the Philippines.

Being both tiny and nocturnal, the chances of finding one in these forests is frankly infinitessimal. Fortunately, help is at hand: the best place to see them is to head to the Tarsier Research and Development Center, a captive breeding site near the village of Corella, just north-east of Tagbilaran. Here, a fenced area of forest is home to a handful of tarsiers, where their keepers will point them out to you – even here you would find it difficult to spot them alone.

For waterfalls, the most impressive and accessible are the Mag Aso Falls, in the west of Bohol and near the town of Antequerra. Cascading through a deep valley, the falls are surrounded by a small area of verdant forest. For further hilly, forested areas, and a chance to explore them, there are the landscapes around the town of Danao, in particular the Danao Adventure Park. This is very much the wild heart of inland Bohol, still only quite lightly trampled by visitors, but rather likely to be increasingly visited in the coming years.

Above: The tiny Philippine Tarsier, the world's smallest primate, is unique to the southern Philippines, and is best seen – as here – at the Tarsier Research and Development Center, near Corella.

Top: The famous Chocolate Hills, near the inland town of Carmen, the iconic Bohol landscape, seen in late afternoon sunlight.

MINDANAO

THE DEEP SOUTH

The Philippines' main southern landmass, Mindanao is probably one of the country's most diverse regions, both culturally and in terms of landscape, and yet it is also one of its least known. The troubles that have traditionally plagued parts of the island have tended to keep visitors away from most of it, ensuring that tourism is, generally speaking, in its infancy, at least in comparison to most of the country.

Despite this, a number of locations in Mindanao's north have become increasingly popular, particularly Siargao and Camiguin Islands, the former the Philippines' premier surfing venue and arguably Mindanao's most popular tourist attraction. The black sand beaches and mountainous volcanic landscape of little Camiguin Island, on the other hand, appeal to those in search of a quiet retreat, exactly what this island provides.

Down in the south, Davao is by far Mindanao's biggest city, though its attractions lie largely in the mountains and forests to the north and west, particularly in and around Mt Apo Natural Park, the country's highest mountain. Over in the west, Zamboanga may still be a difficult place to visit, but it is a beautiful and interesting area that – when peace becomes more certain – deserves to be included in any traveller's itinerary.

Left: A quiet coastal spot; the beach at Santa Monica on the island of Siargao.

CAMIGUIN ISLAND

A VOLCANIC PEARL

Few places in the Philippines are more beautiful than the lovely island of Camiguin, lying in the country's south, perched a short distance off the north coast of Mindanao. Its mountainous slopes are cloaked in almost iridescently green vegetation, whether that be rice plants, coconut palms or natural forest, and its people are among the friendliest and most laidback in an already friendly and relaxed country.

The island's soil is certainly very fertile, the result of repeated volcanic eruptions that down the aeons have created Camiguin. It has been claimed that Camiguin has more volcanoes crowded onto its surface than any other part of the Philippines. Whether that's true or not, the island is made up largely of five mountainous volcanic peaks, the highest Mt Mambajao at 1,552 m (5,090 ft), though only one – Mt Hibok Hibok (1,332 m/4,369 ft) – is presently active. Most of the island is on one steep slope or another, only a relatively narrow coastal plain separating the mountains from the sea. It is along this plain that most people live and where most of the agriculture is possible.

The shore is a mixture of volcanic rock and grey sand beaches, most of the latter stretching along the island's north coast. The only white sand is to be found on White Island, a constantly shifting sandbar just to the north of Camiguin, and around Mantigue Island, a small coral island off the east coast.

Although those relatively small patches of white sand do attract visitors, the large stretches of grey will always ensure that Camiguin will not attract hordes of beach-lovers. But that is just fine, because those visitors who do come here are drawn by the peace, relaxed mood, friendliness of the people and the stunning beauty of the island's landscape. Every vista is dominated by at least one of the island's glowering mountains, on most days their tops firmly embedded in cloud, something that may not sound very encouraging but which adds hugely to Camiguin's beauty, mystique and charm.

Above: White Island is a rare piece of white sand around Camiguin, this shifting sandbar attracting most of the visitors who make it as far as this volcano-dominated island.

Opposite: Agriculture is still the centrepiece of life on Camiguin, rice fields taking up most of what little flat land there is.

EXPLORING CAMIGUIN

Anyone wanting to explore the island has the choice of going up or going around; in other words, either going up into the mountains, or following the coast road. Most of the resorts, and hence accommodation, lie along the north coast, in and around the villages of Agoho, Naasag and Yumbing, on a stretch of coast that lies more or less directly opposite White Island. It is also here that you will find most of Camiguin's grey sand beaches, though in recent years there has been some fairly steady erosion, particularly at Agoho.

A significant number of fishermen work out of this beach, so the sand is littered with their *bancas*. In the late afternoon, this is a good place to come to watch the men prepare their nets, lines and bamboo traps before they head out for a night of fishing. And none of them will object if you lend a shoulder to help push those boats into the water – they are not light! Come back shortly after dawn to watch them return, the crew shaking out their nets and sorting the catch, usually a mix of sardines, flying fish and tuna.

Getting away from the beach and heading inland, Camiguin's main attractions lie on the northern slopes of Mt Hibok-Hibok. Head and shoulders above all else is the stunning Katibawasan Falls, a magnificent sheer 70-m (229-ft) ribbon of water that plunges straight down a cliff and into a natural pool. Not too far away is Ardent Hot Springs, one of the benefits of living on a volcano. Set in forest, the location is lovely, though the pools themselves are a little spoiled by excessive amounts of concrete. Despite this, they are a great place for a relaxing soak.

Beyond these, following a trail that heads off from close to the Falls, it is possible to hike to the summit of Hibok-Hibok. Though blessed with stupendous views – when it is not shrouded in cloud – it is a very steep, sweaty climb, much of it over open, unshaded, volcanic ground.

Travelling instead along the coast leads through a succession of pleasant little coastal villages, many cloaked in coconut palms, fruit groves and forest trees. There are few specific tourist sights as such, just the lovely rural, mountain and coastal views. That said, places worth stopping at include Tangub Hot Spring, an undeveloped shoreline spring that is a mixture of hot volcanic and cold sea water, the temperature varying with the tide. A little further on, just before the village of Bonbon, stands Mt Vulcan, also called the Old Camiguin Volcano, though actually it is Camiguin's newest volcano, created during an earthquake in 1871. Its slopes have been turned into a Stations of the Cross climb, with stunning views from the summit. Directly offshore floats a white cross, marking the site of the Sunken Cemetery, which sank into the sea during that same earthquake. Follow this road and it will take you all round the island, a 64-km (40-mile) loop that will just keep on delivering beautiful Camiguin views.

Right: A group of local men take time out from work to soak in the refreshing waters of forest-shaded Ardent Hot Springs, on the lower slopes of Mt Hibok-Hibok, Camiguin's currently active volcano.

Opposite: The magnificent Katibawasan Falls cascades down a sheer cliff on the verdant slopes of Mt Hibok-Hibok, a few kilometres from Ardent Hot Springs and in the north of Camiguin Island.

Above: A woman of the Yakan minority shows off some of her colourful woven fabrics, produced on a loom such as the one behind her, at the Yakan Weaving Village, in the west of Zamboanga.

Right: A Yakan woman works at a backstrap loom to produce traditional fabrics, at the Yakan Weaving Village.

Above: Thatched gazebos and a small amount of natural beach forest provide welcome shade on the otherwise dazzlingly bright Santa Cruz beach.

Right: A boat from Zamboanga lies anchored beside the beach on Santa Cruz Island, bathed in crystal-clear water.

Opposite: The white sands and turquoise waters of Santa Cruz Island are Zamboanga's star attraction, visited for just a few hours each day mainly by locals, and thankfully still almost wholly undeveloped.

THE CITY

Zamboanga City is not big, its grid of streets radiating from around the harbour inland towards the airport. To the east sits Fort del Pilar, established by the Spanish in the early 1600s, and today restored to house an extensive museum. Its massive walls enclose a series of attractive, white-washed buildings, arranged around a wide plaza, its intact ramparts giving good views across the local area. Built into its eastern outer wall is a shrine to Our Lady of Pilar, consisting simply of an altar and crucifix set into an alcove in the fort's wall, the seating and prayer areas wholly outdoors. In a city in which the Spanish were unable to impose Catholicism, this is the most historic of the Christian sites.

Spain's main legacy here, however, is language. Easily discernible by the sheer number of Spanish signs across the city – far more than in any other Philippine city – this is just a part of the story. The local dialect, called *chabacano*, is actually a Spanish creole language, a mix of Mexican Spanish, native Philippine words and some Malay, minus the complex Spanish grammar.

Just west of the harbour is Plaza Rizal, site of City Hall – not normally something of interest, but here an architecturally significant building dating from the earliest years of American rule. Further west is the Boulevard, a seafront promenade that is a good place to come at sunset, to chill out and to watch the sun sink over the sea.

THE SUBURBS

On moving further away from the city centre so the neighbourhoods become increasingly Islamic. A few kilometres west there is a small market, a great place to see some wonderful fruit and the huge variety of local seafood. Nearby is the Yakan Weaving Village, a centre for weavers of the Yakan cultural minority, a Muslim group that lives primarily on nearby Basilan Island. Initially appearing to be just a collection of a few stalls selling a mix of hand-woven and mass-produced items, behind is a whole compound of homes where the weaving is actually done. At another collection of stalls laden with a mass of very colourful materials, tablecloths, napkins, bags and so on, all designed with Yakan and Muslim motifs, plus a few Islamic knives and trinkets, you can watch women weaving by hand. They use traditional backstrap looms identical to those in Borneo, a very tiring type of loom in which the entire tension is dependent on the weaver leaning back on their strap to keep the material taut.

North-east of the city is the rural village of Taluksangay, site of what may be Zamboanga's most photogenic mosque, with white-washed walls and red domes, surrounded by coconut palms. Set on a tidal creek, the village in which the mosque sits is anything but a typical Philippine village, but instead is absolutely a quintessential Malay *kampung*, its stilted waterside homes almost identical in every respect to their equivalents in Indonesia and Malaysia.

TO THE BEACH

Zamboanga's star attraction is the stunning beach on Santa Cruz Island, a few kilometres offshore from the city, sitting in the Basilan Strait between Zamboanga and Basilan Island. Reached by hired *banca* from Paseo del Mar, an area of cafes next to Fort del Pilar, the beach is open only from early morning until early afternoon. Development on the beach is absolutely minimal – just a few shelters and *nipa* parasols – and is likely to stay that way for quite some time. It is definitely worth the trip for its fine, bright sand and beautiful turquoise water – just remember to bring all your own food and drink; and sunblock.

A few fishing families live on the island, people of the Samal group. They are the keepers of Zamboanga's most famous icon, the *vintas*. Traditional outrigger canoes powered by highly colourful sails, they have become *the* symbol of Zamboanga beyond anything else. Originating from the Badjao people, or sea gypsies, different patterns on the sails originally had different meanings, but inevitably they have fallen out of daily use. In Zamboanga the *vintas* are seen en masse only during the annual Zamboanga regatta, held each October. As a tourism icon, they can sometimes be seen around Paseo del Mar, and for a price the men of Santa Cruz can put on a bit of a *vinta* display. This should be arranged through the *banca*-hiring desk at Paseo del Mar.

A group of *vintas* out on the water is a very colourful sight; definitely an essential part of any visit to Zamboanga.

Above: *Vintas*, Zamboanga's traditional sailing outrigger boats, prepare for a cruise, on Santa Cruz Island.

Opposite: The shrine of Our Lady of Pilar, set into one of the outer walls of Zamboanga's Fort del Pilar, is a wholly outdoor set-up.

ZAMBOANGA

THE FIRST AND LAST CITY

How can anyone not be intrigued by a city with a name as exotic as Zamboanga? It sounds distant, different and colourful, a far-off place you might one day aspire to try to reach. Of course, the reality is a little more prosaic than that: this is a Philippine city much like many other Philippine cities, and it is easy enough to reach by air. But it is, you could say, right at the very end of the line, from the Philippine perspective: sitting at the furthest tip of Mindanao's long, narrow westerly peninsula, as far-removed from the rest of mainland Mindanao as it could possibly be, while still being on the mainland.

Zamboanga is the starting point for the chain of islands that stretch south-westwards across the Sulu Sea, reaching all the way down to both Indonesian and Malaysian Borneo, and from that perspective it is very much the start, not the end of the Philippines. For many hundreds of years, this was a major gateway to the Philippine islands, Islam coming up from Borneo, working its way into the southern Philippines via Zamboanga. Before Islam, the area was also the first landfall for large numbers migrating up from today's Sulu Islands, Indonesia and Malaysia, people who eventually settled across the Philippines to create today's Filipinos.

The city now is a mix of Islamic and Christian cultures, governed as a fully integral part of the Philippines, but surrounded by a largely Islamic, autonomously governed region. As a result, Zamboanga has seen more than its fair share of trouble, as one of the zones of friction between the central Manila government and local Islamic authorities struggling for greater autonomy. And that is a shame, because actually Zamboanga and its area is a lovely place, with some beautiful countryside, fantastic beaches, an intriguing culture and some terrific seafood. It really is a place worth visiting.

DON'T THROW
OBJECTS
THE POND

INDEX

MICROTEL BY WYNDHAM PUERTO PRINCESA
Emerald Beach
San Jose
Puerto Princesa
Palawan 5300
Tel: +63 (0)917 549 7363
Email: puertoprincesa@microtel.ph
Website: www.microtel-palawan.com

THE VISAYAS

ANDA WHITE BEACH RESORT
Sitio Dagohoy
Barangay Bacong
Anda
Bohol 6311
Tel: +63 (0)917 700 0507
Email: reservations@andabeachresort.com
Website: www.andabeachresort.com

AMORITA RESORT
Tawala
1 Ester A Lim Drive
Tawala
Alona Beach
Panglao Island
Bohol 6340
Tel: +63 (0)38 502 9003
Email: inquiries@one-ofcollections.com
Website: www.amoritaresort.com

CORAL CAY RESORT
Solangan
San Juan
Siquijor 6227
Tel: +63 (0)919 269 1269
Website: https://coralcayresortsiquijor.com

DISCOVERY SHORES BORACAY
Station 1
Balabag
Boracay Island
Aklan 5608
Tel: +63 (0)36 288 9689
Email: reservations@dsb.discovery.com.ph
Website: www.discoveryshoresboracay.com

FLORENTINA HOMES
L Rovira Rd
Barangay Bantayan
Dumaguete City
Negros Oriental 6200
Tel: +63 (0)35 522 3778
Email: florentinahomes@yahoo.com
Website: www.florentinahomes.com

HOYOHOY VILLAS
F Roska Street
Santa Fe
Bantayan Island
Cebu 6047
Tel: +63 (0)32 438 9021
Email: info@hoyohoy-villas.com
Website: www.hoyohoy-villas.com

MALAPASCUA EXOTIC ISLAND RESORT
Bounty Beachfront
Sitio Pasil Logon
Malapascua Island
Daan Bantayan
Cebu 6013
Tel: +63 (0)917 307 0150
Email: exoticdivers@gmail.com
Website: www.malapascua.net

SHANGRI-LA'S MACTAN RESORT AND SPA
Punta Engaño Rd
PO Box 86
Lapu-Lapu City
Cebu 6015
Tel: +63 (0)32 231 0288
Email: mactan@shangri-la.com
Website: www.shangri-la.com/cebu/mactanresort

COSTABELLA TROPICAL BEACH HOTEL
Buyong
Mactan Island
Cebu 6015
Tel: +63 (0)32 238 2700
Email: rsvn@costabellaresort.com
Website: https://costabellaresort.com

JANNAH-GLYCEL BEACH HOUSE
Talisay
Nueva Valencia
Guimaras 5046
Tel: +63 (0)33 582 1003
Email: reservation@jannahglycelbeach.com
Website: https://beachnear.me/jannah-glycel-beach-house

INJAP TOWER HOTEL
Diversion Rd
Mandurriao
Iloilo City
Iloilo 5000
Tel: +63 (0)33 330 7111
Email: iloilo@injaptowerhotel.com.ph
Website: www.injaptowerhotel.com.ph

MINDANAO

ROYAL MANDAYA HOTEL DAVAO
J Palma Gil Street
Davao 8000
Tel: +63 (0)82 225 8888
Email: info@theroyalmandayahotel.com
Website: www.theroyalmandayahotel.com

GARDEN ORCHID HOTEL
Gov Camins Ave
Zamboanga City
Zamboanga del Sur 7000
Tel: +63 (0)62 991 0031
Email: gardenorchidhotelzambo@gmail.com
Website: www.gardenorchidhotels.com

ALON RESORT
Barangay Catangnan
General Luna
Siargao Island
Surigao del Norte
Tel: +63 (0)919 999 5854
Email: info@cloud9surf.com
Website: https://alonsiargao.ph

AGOHO RESORT
Agoho, Mambajao
Camiguin Island 9100
Tel: +63 (0)965 718 5878
Email: agohoresort@gmail.com
Website: https://agohoresort.com

FURTHER INFORMATION

Below is a list of accommodation suggestions for many of the places visited in this book.

LUZON

GOLDEN PHOENIX HOTEL MANILA
Oceanaire Building
Sunrise Drive
Central Business Park
Diosdado Macapagal
Pasay City
Metro Manila 1300
Tel: +63 (0)2 8683 2888
Email: reservations@goldenphoenixhotelmanila.com
Website: www.goldenphoenixhotelmanila.com

DIAMOND HOTEL
Roxas Boulevard cor Dr J Quintos St
Manila 1000
Tel: +63 (0)2 8528 3000
Email: guestservices@diamondhotel.com
Website: www.diamondhotel.com

VILLA ANGELA
26 Quirino Boulevard
Vigan
Ilocos Sur
Tel: +63 (0)77 722 2914
Email: villangela.heritage@gmail.com
Website: https://ourheritagehomes.com/listing/villa-angela-heritage-house

THE LITTLE SURFMAID RESORT
170 Urbiztondo
San Juan
La Union 2514
Tel: +63 (0)72 619 2196
Email: surfmaid@gmail.com
Website: https://surfmaid.wixsite.com/surfmaid

ISLAND TROPIC HOTEL
Boulevard St
Barangay Lucap
Alaminos City
Pangasinan 2404
Tel: +63 (0)75 211 9939
Email: info@islandtropichotel.com
Website: https://islandtropichotel.com

THE MANOR AT CAMP JOHN HAY
Ordonio Drive
Baguio City
Benguet 2600
Tel: +63 (0)74 424 0931
Email: reservations@campjohnhay.ph
Website: https://campjohnhay.ph

BANAUE HOTEL AND YOUTH HOSTEL
Ilogue
Banaue
Mountain province
Tel: +63 (0)927 570 2355 (mobile/cell phone)
Email: banauehotel@tieza.gov.ph
Website: https://banauehotelandyouthhostel.com

COSTA PACIFICA
80 Buton St
Sitio Labasin
Barangay Sabang
Baler
Aurora 3200
Tel: +63 (0)917 844 8371
Email: resa@costapacificabaler.com
Website: www.costapacificabaler.com

TAAL VISTA HOTEL
Kilometer 60
Aguinaldo Highway
Tagaytay City 4120
Tel: +63 (0)46 413 1000
Email: reservations@taalvistahotel.com
Website: www.taalvistahotel.com

ORIENTAL HOTEL LEGAZPI
Taysan Hill
Santo Nino Village
Legazpi City
Albay 4500
Tel: +63 (0)998 999 0865
Email: inquiry@theorientalhotels.com
Website: https://legazpi.theorientalhotels.com

MINDORO

MARCO VINCENT DIVE RESORT
White Beach
Puerto Galera
Oriental Mindoro 5203
Tel: +63 (0)918 957 4459
Email: mvresort@marcovincent.com
Website: www.marcovincent.com

PALAWAN

CLUB PARADISE
Dimakya Island
Coron
Palawan 5316
Tel: +63(0)2 7719 6971
Email: reservations@cp.discovery.com.ph
Website: www.clubparadisepalawan.com

LAGEN ISLAND RESORT
El Nido
Palawan 5313
Tel: +63 (0)2 7902 5980
Email: holiday@elnidoresorts.com
Website: www.elnidoresorts.com